The Outbreak of the First World War

PROBLEMS IN
EUROPEAN CIVILIZATION

Under the editorial direction of
John Ratté
Amherst College

The
Outbreak of the
First World War

Causes and Responsibilities
Fourth Edition

Edited and with an introduction by

Dwight E. Lee
Clark University, Emeritus

D. C. HEATH AND COMPANY
Lexington, Massachusetts Toronto

CONTENTS

I WHO OR WHAT CAUSED WAR?

II THE GERMAN WAR-GUILT QUESTION REVIVED

III NEW PERSPECTIVES ON THE OUTBREAK OF THE WAR

INTRODUCTION

The origins of the First World War have become a major historical problem not merely because the event seemed to be of great significance as a turning point in world history, but also, and perhaps more importantly, because the question of who was responsible, raised during the war and answered in the peace settlement, became a vital and passionately argued issue in both domestic and international politics.

By placing the blame for the war on Germany and its allies and thereby justifying reparations, the victorious powers supplied one of the major factors utilized by Hitler in his rise to power in Germany. The reaction to the Versailles verdict which occurred in the victorious countries as well as in Germany resulted in an attack upon Article 231 of the Versailles treaty in the name of "revisionism." Thus there arose a battle whose front extended from newspapers and popular magazines, through the offices of propagandists and politicians and the quieter studies of scholarly historians, to the halls of parliaments and the green baize tables of international conferences. By the middle of the 1930s the excited conflict of opinion had cooled down and the issues had receded into the background of political discussion as reparations payments stopped and Hitler achieved revision. The study of the problem, however, has inevitably continued, albeit at a slower and soberer pace until the revival of the war-guilt question in Germany in 1961 again created a furor in the historical world.

Before coming to that third phase of the problem, some general considerations are worth noting. First of all, for the historian the judgment of the peacemakers proved to be a boon because the Germans immediately undertook to refute the charges against their nation by publishing a huge collection of documents from their foreign office archives covering the period from 1871 to 1914. Since this action could not go unchallenged, other governments had to follow the German example and produce their records. As a result, and even though the publications of Italy and Russia are still incomplete, the historian has had at his disposal a vast store of primary source material with which to work. Thus, when normally the scholar would have had to wait at least a hundred years to get at the secrets of government offices, he has been embarrassed with the riches of documentary evidence for the backgrounds of the First World War. Of course, the first decade of the "revisionist" battle was fought without the complete body of primary sources, and that is one reason why study must go on if we are ever to assess the evidence and draw conclusions fairly.

Another reason for the continued study of this, as of other historical problems, is that viewpoints change and with them the questions which historians seek to answer. Article 231 of Versailles fixed the searchlight of the 1920s upon the question "Who was guilty?" As the smoke of the revisionist battle gradually drifted away, it became obvious that this was not a proper question for the historian because the answer would scarcely contribute to a better understanding of historical processes or help us to improve the chances of peaceful development today. For, even if Germany were guilty in 1914, it would be absurd to believe, especially after 1947, that by punishing and fettering Germany we could prevent war. As time went on, therefore, more and more attention was devoted to such questions as "What were the conditions that made war possible?" and "Why, when so many crises were solved peaceably before 1914, did the one in July 1914 end in war?" The answers to such questions depend not only upon the bare record of the documents and other evidence, but also upon the conscious or unconscious assumptions the student makes about economic, political, intellectual, and social forces in the formulation of policy and the making of decisions by national governments. These assumptions help to determine what the historian will select and what he will reject from the overwhelming mass of evidence, and they also help to determine what interpretation he will put upon the wording of his documents.

In the space available in the following pages it is impossible to reproduce all the key documents, even for the short period of less than a month in the 1914 crisis that ended in war. Nor is it possible to give detailed interpretations of the exchanges that took place among the statesmen involved, for the most thorough studies run to volumes rather than pages. Therefore the selection of readings has been made in order to give (1) something of the flavor of the revisionist debate at its height in the twenties, and the principal viewpoints that emerged in subsequent decades; (2) a sample of the heated German controversy that arose in the sixties over German guilt; and (3) viewpoints representing the perspective of recent times. The Suggestions for Additional Reading at the end of this book will give some guidance to those who would like to get beneath the surface and examine the evidence for themselves.

Under Part I the report of 1919 made to the peace conference on the responsibility for the war appropriately begins the selection of readings, not only because it was the basis for Article 231 of the Versailles treaty, but also because it reflects the inevitably one-sided approach of the victors to the question of guilt as well as the comparative paucity of sources on which their judgment was based. The excerpt from Sidney Bradshaw Fay's *Origins* represents the more balanced conclusions of a leading revisionist scholar and the more judicious temper of the late 1920s compared to the earlier polemical tone. On the other hand, Harry Elmer Barnes sets forth the extreme revisionist view held in the United States, Germany, France, and Great Britain. George Peabody Gooch, publishing in the late 1930s with the advantage of a fuller body of sources than was available to either Barnes or Fay, refutes the former's picture of a Poincaré bent upon war and assesses Bethmann Hollweg's miscalculations and inadequacies.

Another kind of extreme revisionism from that of Barnes has existed since the early days of the First World War—the Marxist interpretation. Although the extract from K. Zilliacus, a British left-wing parliamentarian and writer, is not as violent or dogmatic as many of the Marxists have been, it nevertheless gives the view that the war is to be explained by economic rivalries, class interests, and the machinations of finance capital. On the other hand, there has emerged a counter-Marxist trend that discounts the importance of economic factors or denies the validity of economic determinism.

Pierre Renouvin, the leading French historian of international affairs, while recognizing the importance of economic and social factors, not only throws doubt upon the notion that capitalist competition caused the war, but also calls attention to the personal element in diplomacy as well as to nationalism and the passions it aroused.

Finally, Raymond Aron well conveys the atmosphere of research in the fifties, and makes clear the position of the scholarly student for whom 1914 and its background is no simple picture but rather one of great complexity from which storybook villains are absent. He is not saying, however, that there is no problem for the student in the outbreak of the war, but rather that the reduction of general and immediate causes to black-and-white terms, to "guilty" and "guiltless," is to miss the point. There was no inevitable trend of events toward war, but rather the acts of sovereign states seeking what seemed to them at the time to be in their best interest. Alliances and armaments, pursued for defense, proved to be the means of creating tension; the nationalist ambition of a small Balkan state, backed by a great power, threatened the existence of an historic empire, supported by another great power. The alliances and alignments guaranteed that the crisis would be Europe-wide. In this situation, the decisions of Austria-Hungary and Germany on the one hand, and of Russia on the other, involved fateful consequences.

In Part II, three statements illustrate the revived war-guilt debate, but before commenting upon them, something of the background needs to be sketched. The first full-length and thoroughly documented reassertion of German war guilt was published in three volumes by Luigi Albertini, Italian journalist and senator, in 1942–1943. His work was translated into English and edited by Isabella M. Massey as *The Origins of the War of 1914*, in three volumes, 1952–1957. Neither the Italian nor the English edition was taken seriously in Germany until Fritz Fischer, first in a periodical article and then in his book, *Griff nach der Weltmacht* [*Grab for World Power*], in 1961 startled the German historical profession and public by affirming Albertini's conclusion that Germany was guilty of starting the war, as part of his exposition of Germany's aggressive imperialist war aims. The impact of his book can be understood only if we recall that German innocence and the notion that Germany had fought defensively in the war had become truths that no German before had dared to challenge. The furor that arose over Fischer's position has been dubbed the "Fischer controversy."[1] Thus, Fischer's interpretation of Germany's responsibility for the outbreak of the war in 1914 appropriately opens Part II on "German War Guilt Revived." His exposition parallels, but lacks the fullness and richness of detail of Albertini's study which, unfortunately, does not lend itself to excerpting for reproduction here.

Three groups of German critics and commentators who have participated in the "Fischer controversy" may be distinguished: those who cling to the traditional view of German innocence and flatly deny the validity of Fischer's thesis; those who fully accept and expand upon it; and those who admit that the older war-guilt literature needs revision, but reject Fischer's reconstruction of the July crisis. Among the last is Gerhard Ritter, one of whose critical reviews of Fischer's book is reprinted in part below. He contends that Fischer has misinterpreted the sources in his determination to prove a thesis, but does not attempt to offer a full-length exposition of his own.

Thus far, aside from a few pieces of newly discovered source material, the German controversy has not significantly added to the substance of the debate or changed the issues and viewpoints concerning the outbreak of the war that emerged in the literature of the twenties and thirties, excepting, perhaps, to cast Bethmann Hollweg in a new light—a point that the Ritter selection briefly touches upon, and is taken up in detail by Konrad H. Jarausch with the aid of the Riezler diary, mentioned by Fischer, and archival material hitherto unused. While Jarausch does not controvert Fischer's statement of Bethmann's aims in the July crisis—or Gooch's assessment of him—his emphasis is quite different. He sees Bethmann not as an aggressive imperialist, but as a traditional nationalist seeking German security and greatness.

The excerpts in Part III deal in different ways with the broad question of how to approach the outbreak of war, and incidentally participate in the Fischer controversy. Arno J. Mayer pleads for a wider base than that of the exclusively diplomatic approach to the war, arguing that the domestic situation in each of the great powers

[1] For a short summary of the controversy and the personalities involved, see Imanuel Geiss, *July 1914* (New York, 1967), pp. 9–15; and for a description of the means by which the German foreign office had promoted the revisionist thesis in the 1920s, see Geiss, "Outbreak of the First World War and German War Aims," *Journal of Contemporary History* 1 (1966): 75–79; or *1914*, edited by Walter Laqueur and George L. Mosse (New York, 1966), pp. 71–77.

must be taken into account. Joachim Remak interprets 1914 as a continuation of the Balkan wars that had almost brought a European war in 1912–1913. Paul W. Schroeder, on the other hand, breaks out of the pattern of approaches to the First World War hitherto pursued and asks not "Why the War?" but "Why not?" His essay might well be taken as the starting point for a wholly new perspective that would enable the student the better to follow Raymond Aron's advice not to seek criminals, but rather the significance and the roots of the war.

The challenge presented by the First World War to the student historian therefore still remains. In examining the conflict of opinion represented in the selections offered here and pursuing his study further, he may find his inquiry more meaningful if he asks himself such questions as these: Upon what assumptions and within what frames of reference were the statesmen of 1914 making their decisions? What were the choices before them? Why did they make the decisions that they did? Given the system of independent, sovereign national states, each seeking ultimately its own security and well-being, could greater intelligence, more determination to avoid the risks of war, or speedier and franker statements of positions have averted bloodshed? Or were the issues such that they could not be resolved by peaceful means because they touched upon "vital" national interests? And, despite Aron and others, were there "villains" after all?

Principal Proper Names

Aehrenthal, Alois, Baron (later, Count) Lexa: Austro-Hungarian Minister for Foreign Affairs, 1906–1912.

Ballplatz [Ballhausplatz]: Site in Vienna of the Ministry of Foreign Affairs and hence a synonym for it.

Berchtold, Leopold, Count von: Austro-Hungarian Minister for Foreign Affairs, February 1912–1915.

Bethmann Hollweg, Dr. Theobald von: German Chancellor, 1909–1917.

Bülow, Bernhard, Prince von: German Chancellor, 1900–1909.

Bunsen, Sir Maurice de: British Ambassador in Vienna, 1913–1914.

Cambon, Jules: French Ambassador in Berlin, 1907–1914.

Carol I: King of Rumania, 1881–1914.

Chamberlain, Joseph: British Secretary for the Colonies, 1895–1903.

Conrad von Hoetzendorf, Franz, Baron (later, Count) von: Austro-Hungarian Chief of the General Staff, 1906–1911, 1912–1917.

Crowe, Sir Eyre: Senior Clerk (later, Assistant Undersecretary at the British Foreign Office), 1906–1920.

Delcassé, Théophile: French Minister for Foreign Affairs, 1898–1905; Ambassador to Russia, 1913–1914.

Dobrorolski, General Sergei Konstantinovich: Chief of the Mobilization Section of the Russian General Staff, 1914.

Falkenhayn, General Erich G.A.S. von: Prussian Minister of War, 1914.

Francis [Franz] Ferdinand, Archduke: Austro-Hungarian heir apparent, 1896–1914.

Francis [Franz] Joseph: Emperor of Austria, 1848–1916; and King of Hungary, 1867–1916.

Grey, Sir Edward (later, Viscount Grey of Fallodon): British Secretary for Foreign Affairs, 1905–1916.

Hoyos, Alexander, Count: Chief of Berchtold's Cabinet, 1914.

Izvolsky [Iswolski], Alexander Petrovich: Russian Foreign Minister, 1906–1910; Ambassador to France, 1910–1917.

Jagow, Gottlieb von: German Secretary for Foreign Affairs, 1913–1916.

Lichnowsky, Karl Max, Prince von: German Ambassador in London, 1912–1914.

Moltke, General Helmuth J. L. von: Chief of the German General Staff, 1906–1914.

Nicolson, Sir Arthur (later, Lord Carnock): British Ambassador to Russia, 1906–1910; Permanent Undersecretary for Foreign Affairs, 1910–1916.

Paléologue, Maurice: French Ambassador to Russia, 1914–1917.

Pashich [Pašić] Nikola: Serbian Prime Minister, 1912–1919.

Poincaré, Raymond: French Premier, 1912–1913; President, 1913–1920.

Quai d'Orsay: Site in Paris of the Ministry of Foreign Affairs and hence a synonym for it.

Riezler, Kurt: Assistant and confidant of Bethmann Hollweg.

San Giuliano, Antonino, Marquis of: Italian Minister for Foreign Affairs, 1910–1914.

Sazonov [Sazonoff], Sergei Dimitrievich: Russian Minister for Foreign Affairs, 1910–1916.

Schoen, Wilhelm Eduard, Baron von: German Ambassador to France, 1910–1914.

Sukhomlinov, General Vladimir Alexandrovich: Russian Minister of War, 1909–1915.

Szögényi, Laszlo, Count: Austro-Hungarian Ambassador in Berlin, 1892–1914.

Tirpitz, Admiral Alfred von: German Navy Minister, 1898–1916.

Tisza, Stephen, Count: Hungarian Premier, 1913–1917.

Tschirschky und Bögendorff, Heinrich Leonhard von: German Ambassador in Vienna, 1907–1916.

Viviani, René: French Premier and Minister for Foreign Affairs, June–August 1914.

Wilhelmstrasse: Site in Berlin of the German Foreign Office and hence a synonym for it.

Wolff, Theodor: Editor of the *Berliner Tageblatt,* 1914.

Zimmermann, Arthur: German Undersecretary for Foreign Affairs, 1911–1916.

Conflict of Opinion

Germany and her allies were the aggressors:

> The Allied and Associated Governments affirm and Germany accepts the responsibility of Germany and her allies for causing all the loss and damage to which the Allied and Associated Governments and their nationals have been subjected as a consequence of the war imposed upon them by the aggression of Germany and her allies.
>
> ARTICLE 231 OF THE TREATY OF VERSAILLES

France and Russia willed the war:

> The Franco-Russian Alliance concluded by 1894 was transformed into an offensive organization following 1912 through the cooperation of Izvolski and Poincaré. Both recognized that the chief objects of Russian and French foreign policy, the seizure of the Straits and the return of Alsace-Lorraine, could be realized only through a general European war.... When the assassination [of Francis Ferdinand] came, the French and Russians recognized that the impending clash between Austria and Serbia would constitute a highly appropriate episode over which to bring about the desired conflict.... In estimating the order of guilt of the various countries we may safely say that the only direct and immediate responsibility for the World War falls upon Serbia, France and Russia, with the guilt about equally distributed.
>
> HARRY ELMER BARNES

Socioeconomic causes of the war:

> If there is one lesson ... it is the almost unbelievable blindness, tenacity, cruelty, and unscrupulousness with which the governing classes cling to their privileges and power at any cost to their suffering peoples and to the wider interests of peace and civilization.
>
> K. ZILLIACUS

Nationalism the dominant factor:

> In fact, the conflict occurred only at the moment when political considerations—concern for safeguarding security or the desire for power —clashed violently.... The effective impulsion came from national feeling and from passionate emotions.
>
> PIERRE RENOUVIN

No criminals, either men or nations:

> The inquiry into political responsibility carries with it no authority to banish as criminals either men or nations. But inquiry does clarify the significance and the origins of the war.
>
> RAYMOND ARON

German responsibility for war in 1914:

> As Germany willed and coveted the Austro-Serbian war and, in her confidence in her military superiority, deliberately faced the risk of a conflict with Russia and France, her leaders must bear a substantial share of the historical responsibility for the outbreak of general war in 1914.
>
> FRITZ FISCHER

Not "Why?" but "Why not?":

> ... The search for the fundamental cause of World War I is futile, while the argument that the war simply happened is unhelpful. Is there no exit from the cul-de-sac? A different question may help: not Why World War I? but Why not? War was still the *ultima ratio regum*. World War I was a normal development in international relations; events had been building toward it for a long time. There is no need to explain it as a deviation from the norm. In this sense, the question Why not? answers the question Why?
>
> PAUL W. SCHROEDER

I WHO OR WHAT CAUSED WAR?

Commission on War Guilt

REPORT PRESENTED TO THE PRELIMINARY PEACE CONFERENCE (1919)

"The Commission on the Responsibility of the Authors of the War and on Enforcement of Penalties," to give its full title, was created at the plenary session of the Paris Peace Conference of January 25, 1919. Two representatives of each of the five Great Powers (The United States, France, Great Britain, Italy, and Japan) and one each from Belgium, Greece, Poland, Rumania, and Serbia made up its membership. United States Secretary of State Robert Lansing was chosen chairman of the commission, which made its report toward the end of March. The conference, at its plenary session of May 6, 1919, unanimously adopted the report, although both the United States and Japan added reservations. Only the first chapter of the report has been reprinted below. Most of the sources used as a basis for the report are documents, often carefully edited, which the belligerents issued in the various "color books" shortly after the outbreak of the war.

On the question of the responsibility of the authors of the war, the Commission, after having examined a number of official documents relating to the origin of the World War, and to the violations of neutrality and of frontiers which accompanied its inception, has determined that the responsibility for it lies wholly upon the Powers which declared war in pursuance of a policy of aggression, the concealment of which gives to the origin of this war the character of a dark conspiracy against the peace of Europe.

This responsibility rests first on Germany and Austria, secondly on Turkey and Bulgaria. The responsibility is made all the graver by reason of the violation by Germany and Austria of the neutrality of Belgium and Luxemburg, which they themselves had guaranteed. It is increased, with regard to both France and Serbia, by the violation of their frontiers before the declaration of war.

Premeditation of the War: Germany and Austria

Many months before the crisis of 1914 the German Emperor had ceased to pose as the champion of peace. Naturally believing in the

From the *German White Book Concerning the Responsibility of the Authors of the War* (New York, 1924), pp. 15–21. Used with the permission of the Carnegie Endowment for International Peace. Footnotes omitted.

overwhelming superiority of his Army, he openly showed his enmity towards France. General von Moltke said to the King of the Belgians: "This time the matter must be settled." In vain the King protested. The Emperor and his Chief of Staff remained no less fixed in their attitude.

On the 28th of June, 1914, occurred the assassination at Serajevo of the heir-apparent of Austria. "It is the act of a little group of madmen," said Francis Joseph. The act, committed as it was by a subject of Austria-Hungary on Austro-Hungarian territory, could in no wise compromise Serbia, which very correctly expressed its condolences and stopped public rejoicings in Belgrade. If the Government of Vienna thought that there was any Serbian complicity, Serbia was ready to seek out the guilty parties. But this attitude failed to satisfy Austria and still less Germany, who, after their first astonishment had passed, saw in this royal and national misfortune a pretext to initiate war.

At Potsdam a "decisive consultation" took place on the 5th of July, 1914. Vienna and Berlin decided upon this plan: "Vienna will send to Belgrade a very emphatic ultimatum with a very short limit of time."

The Bavarian Minister, von Lerchenfeld, said in a confidential dispatch dated the 18th of July, 1914, the facts stated in which have never been officially denied: "It is clear that Serbia cannot accept the demands, which are inconsistent with the dignity of an independent state." Count Lerchenfeld reveals in this report that, at the time it was made, the ultimatum to Serbia had been jointly decided upon by the Governments of Berlin and Vienna; that they were waiting to send it until President Poincaré and Mr. Viviani should have left for St. Petersburg; and that no illusions were cherished, either at Berlin or Vienna, as to the consequences which this threatening measure would involve. It was perfectly well known that war would be the result.

The Bavarian Minister explains, moreover, that the only fear of the Berlin Government was that Austria-Hungary might hesitate and draw back at the last minute, and that on the other hand Serbia, on the advice of France and Great Britain, might yield to the pressure put upon her. Now, "the Berlin Government considers that war is necessary." Therefore, it gave full powers to Count Berchtold, who instructed the Ballplatz on the 18th of July, 1914, to negotiate with

Bulgaria to induce her to enter into an alliance and to participate in the war.

In order to mask this understanding, it was arranged that the Emperor should go for a cruise in the North Sea, and that the Prussian Minister of War should go for a holiday, so that the Imperial Government might pretend that events had taken it completely by surprise.

Austria suddenly sent Serbia an ultimatum that she had carefully prepared in such a way as to make it impossible to accept. Nobody could be deceived; "the whole world understands that this ultimatum means war." According to Mr. Sazonoff, "Austria-Hungary wanted to devour Serbia."

Mr. Sazonoff asked Vienna for an extension of the short time-limit of forty-eight hours given by Austria to Serbia for the most serious decision in its history. Vienna refused the demand. On the 24th and 25th of July, England and France multiplied their efforts to persuade Serbia to satisfy the Austro-Hungarian demands. Russia threw in her weight on the side of conciliation.

Contrary to the expectation of Austria-Hungary and Germany, Serbia yielded. She agreed to all the requirements of the ultimatum, subject to the single reservation that, in the judicial inquiry which she would commence for the purpose of seeking out the guilty parties, the participation of Austrian officials would be kept within the limits assigned by international law. "If the Austro-Hungarian Government is not satisfied with this," Serbia declared she was ready "to submit to the decision of the Hague Tribunal."

"A quarter of an hour before the expiration of the time limit," at 5:45 on the 25th, Mr. Pashitch, the Serbian Minister for Foreign Affairs, delivered this reply to Baron Giesl, the Austro-Hungarian Minister.

On Mr. Pashitch's return to his own office he found awaiting him a letter from Baron Giesl saying that he was not satisfied with the reply. At 6:30 the latter had left Belgrade, and even before he had arrived at Vienna, the Austro-Hungarian Government had handed his passports to Mr. Yovanovitch, the Serbian Minister, and had prepared thirty-three mobilization proclamations, which were published on the following morning in the *Budapesti Kozlöni,* the official gazette of the Hungarian Government. On the 27th Sir Maurice de Bunsen telegraphed to Sir Edward Grey: "This country has gone wild with joy at the prospect of war with Serbia." At midday on the

28th Austria declared war on Serbia. On the 29th the Austrian army commenced the bombardment of Belgrade, and made its dispositions to cross the frontier.

The reiterated suggestions of the Entente Powers with a view to finding a peaceful solution of the dispute only produced evasive replies on the part of Berlin or promises of intervention with the Government of Vienna without any effectual steps being taken.

On the 24th of July Russia and England asked that the Powers should be granted a reasonable delay in which to work in concert for the maintenance of peace. Germany did not join in this request.

On the 25th of July Sir Edward Grey proposed mediation by four Powers (England, France, Italy and Germany). France and Italy immediately gave their concurrence. Germany refused, alleging that it was not a question of mediation but of arbitration, as the conference of the four Powers was called to make proposals, not to decide.

On the 26th of July Russia proposed to negotiate directly with Austria. Austria refused.

On the 27th of July England proposed a European conference. Germany refused.

On the 29th of July Sir Edward Grey asked the Wilhelmstrasse to be good enough to "suggest any method by which the influence of the four Powers could be used together to prevent a war between Austria and Russia." She was asked herself to say what she desired. Her reply was evasive.

On the same day, the 29th of July, the Czar dispatched to the Emperor William II a telegram suggesting that the Austro-Serbian problem should be submitted to the Hague Tribunal. This suggestion received no reply. This important telegram does not appear in the German White Book. It was made public by the Petrograd *Official Gazette* (January, 1915).

The Bavarian Legation, in a report dated the 31st of July, declared its conviction that the efforts of Sir Edward Grey to preserve peace would not hinder the march of events.

As early as the 21st of July German mobilization had commenced by the recall of a certain number of classes of the reserve, then of German officers in Switzerland, and finally of the Metz garrison on the 25th of July. On the 26th of July the German fleet was called back from Norway.

The Entente did not relax its conciliatory efforts, but the German Government systematically brought all its attempts to nought. When Austria consented for the first time on the 31st of July to discuss the contents of the Serbian note with the Russian Government and the Austro-Hungarian Ambassador received orders to "converse" with the Russian Minister of Foreign Affairs, Germany made any negotiation impossible by sending her ultimatum to Russia. Prince Lichnowsky wrote that "a hint from Berlin would have been enough to decide Count Berchtold to content himself with a diplomatic success and to declare that he was satisfied with the Serbian reply, but this hint was not given. *On the contrary they went forward towards war.*"

On the 1st of August the German Emperor addressed a telegram to the King of England containing the following sentence: "The troops on my frontier are, at this moment, being kept back by telegraphic and telephonic orders from crossing the French frontier." Now, war was not declared till two days after that date, and as the German mobilization orders were issued on that same day, the 1st of August, it follows that, as a matter of fact, the German Army had been mobilized and concentrated in pursuance of previous orders.

The attitude of the Entente nevertheless remained still to the very end so conciliatory that, at the very time at which the German fleet was bombarding Libau, Nicholas II gave his word of honor to William II that Russia would not undertake any aggressive action during the *pourparlers,* and that when the German troops commenced their march across the French frontier Mr. Viviani telegraphed to all the French Ambassadors "we must not stop working for accommodation."

On the 3d of August Mr. von Schoen went to the Quai d'Orsay with the declaration of war against France. Lacking a real cause of complaint, Germany alleged, in her declaration of war, that bombs had been dropped by French airplanes in various districts in Germany. This statement was entirely false. Moreover, it was either later admitted to be so or no particulars were ever furnished by the German Government.

Moreover, in order to be manifestly above reproach, France was careful to withdraw her troops ten kilometers from the German frontier. Notwithstanding this precaution, numerous officially established violations of French territory preceded the declaration of war.

The provocation was so flagrant that Italy, herself a member of the Triple Alliance, did not hesitate to declare that in view of the aggressive character of the war the *casus foederis* ceased to apply.

Conclusions

1. *The war was premeditated by the Central Powers together with their Allies, Turkey and Bulgaria, and was the result of acts deliberately committed in order to make it unavoidable.*
2. *Germany, in agreement with Austria-Hungary, deliberately worked to defeat all the many conciliatory proposals made by the Entente Powers and their repeated efforts to avoid war.*

Sidney Bradshaw Fay

ORIGINS OF THE WORLD WAR

While the revisionist battle was raging on all fronts, from the daily press to scholarly conferences and journals, and new revelations were ever bursting into print to furnish fresh ammunition for both sides, Professor Fay set to work quietly and systematically to rewrite the diplomatic backgrounds of the war and to unravel the tangled story of the 1914 crisis. His Origins of the World War, *which appeared in 1928, was the first major work by an American historian to attempt a sober analysis of the whole problem, and immediately put him in the front ranks of the moderate revisionists who were now more concerned with critical judgment than with polemical acumen. His conclusions, reprinted below, have stood the test of time remarkably well, despite the additional sources and the changes in emphasis that have occurred since 1928.*

None of the Powers wanted a European War. Their governing rulers and ministers, with very few exceptions, all foresaw that it must be a frightful struggle, in which the political results were not absolutely certain, but in which the loss of life, suffering, and economic consequences were bound to be terrible. This is true, in a greater or

From Sidney Bradshaw Fay, *Origins of the World War*, Second Edition (II, pp. 547–558). Copyright 1930 by Macmillan Publishing Co., Inc., and 1958 by Sidney Bradshaw Fay. Reprinted with permission of Macmillan Publishing Co., Inc.

ˑless degree, of Pashitch, Berchtold, Bethmann, Sazonoff, Poincaré, San Giuliano and Sir Edward Grey. Yet none of them, not even Sir Edward Grey, could have foreseen that the political results were to be so stupendous, and the other consequences so terrible, as was actually the case.

For many of the Powers, to be sure, a European War might seem to hold out the possibility of achieving various desired advantages: for Serbia, the achievement of national unity for all Serbs; for Austria, the revival of her waning prestige as a Great Power, and the checking of nationalistic tendencies which threatened her very existence; for Russia, the accomplishment of her historic mission of controlling Constantinople and the Straits; for Germany, new economic advantages and the restoration of the European balance which had changed with the weakening of the Triple Alliance and the tightening of the Triple Entente; for France, the recovery of Alsace-Lorraine and the ending of the German menace; and for England, the destruction of the German naval danger and of Prussian militarism. All these advantages, and many others, were feverishly striven and intrigued for, on all sides, the moment the War actually broke out, but this is no good proof that any of the statesmen mentioned deliberately aimed to bring about a war to secure these advantages. One cannot judge the motives which actuated men before the War, by what they did in an absolutely new situation which arose as soon as they were overtaken by a conflagration they had sought to avert. And in fact, in the case of the two Powers between whom the immediate conflict arose, the postponement or avoidance of a European War would have facilitated the accomplishment of the ultimate advantages aimed at: Pashitch knew that there was a better chance for Serbian national unity after he had consolidated Serbian gains in the Balkan Wars, and after Russia had completed her military and naval armaments as planned for 1917; and Berchtold knew that he had a better chance of crushing the Greater Serbia danger and strengthening Austria, if he could avoid Russian intervention and a general European War. . . .

Nevertheless, a European War broke out. Why? Because in each country political and military leaders did certain things which led to mobilizations and declarations of war, or failed to do certain things which might have prevented them. In this sense, all the European countries, in a greater or less degree, were responsible. One must abandon the dictum of the Versailles Treaty that Germany and her allies were solely responsible. It was a dictum exacted by victors from vanquished, under the influence of the blindness, ignorance, hatred, and the propagandist misconceptions to which war had given rise. It was based on evidence which was incomplete and not always sound. It is generally recognized by the best historical scholars in all countries to be no longer tenable or defensible. They are agreed that the responsibility for the War is a divided responsibility. But they still disagree very much as to the relative part of this responsibility that falls on each country and on each individual political or military leader.

Some writers like to fix positively in some precise mathematical fashion the exact responsibility for the War. This was done in one way by the framers of Article 231 of the Treaty of Versailles. It has been done in other ways by those who would fix the responsibility in some relative fashion, as, for instance, Austria first, then Russia, France and Germany and England. But the present writer deprecates such efforts to assess by a precise formula a very complicated question, which is after all more a matter of delicate shading than of definite white and black. Oversimplification, as Napoleon once said in framing his Code, is the enemy of precision. Moreover, even supposing that a general consensus of opinion might be reached as to the relative responsibility of any individual country or man for immediate causes connected with the July crisis of 1914, it is by no means necessarily true that the same relative responsibility would hold for the underlying causes, which for years had been tending toward the creation of a dangerous situation.

One may, however, sum up very briefly the most salient facts in regard to each country.

Serbia felt a natural and justifiable impulse to do what so many other countries had done in the nineteenth century—to bring under one national Government all the discontented Serb people. She had liberated those under Turkish rule; the next step was to liberate those under Hapsburg rule. She looked to Russia for assistance, and had been encouraged to expect that she would receive it. After the assassination, Mr. Pashitch took no steps to discover and bring to justice Serbians in Belgrade who had been implicated in the plot. One of them, Ciganovitch, was even assisted to disappear. Mr. Pashitch waited to see what evidence the Austrian authorities could find. When Austria demanded cooperation of Austrian officials in discovering, though not in trying, implicated Serbians, the Serbian Government made a very conciliatory but negative reply. They expected that the reply would not be regarded as satisfactory, and, even before it was given, ordered the mobilization of the Serbian army. Serbia did not want war, but believed it would be forced upon her. That Mr. Pashitch was aware of the plot three weeks before it was executed, failed to take effective steps to prevent the assassins from crossing over from Serbia to Bosnia, and then failed to give Austria any warning or information which might have averted the fatal crime, were facts unknown to Austria in July, 1914; they cannot therefore be regarded as in any way justifying Austria's conduct; but they are part of Serbia's responsibility, and a very serious part.

Austria was more responsible for the immediate origin of the war than any other Power. Yet from her own point of view she was acting in self-defense—not against an immediate military attack, but against the corroding Greater Serbia and Jugoslav agitation which her leaders believed threatened her very existence. No State can be expected to sit with folded arms and await dismemberment at the hands of its neighbors. Russia was believed to be intriguing with Serbia and Rumania against the Dual Monarchy. The assassination of the heir to the throne, as a result of a plot prepared in Belgrade, demanded severe retribution; otherwise Austria would be regarded as incapable of action, "wormeaten" as the Serbian Press expressed it, would sink in prestige, and hasten her own downfall. To avert this Berchtold determined to crush Serbia with war. He deliberately framed the ultimatum with the expectation and hope that it would be rejected. He hurriedly declared war against Serbia in order to forestall all efforts at mediation. He refused even to answer his own ally's urgent requests to come to an understanding with Russia, on the basis of a military occupation of Belgrade as a pledge that Serbia would carry out the promises in her reply to the ultimatum. Berchtold gambled on a "local" war with Serbia only, believing that he could rattle the German sword; but rather than abandon his war with Serbia, he was ready to drag the rest of Europe into war.

It is very questionable whether Berchtold's obstinate determination to diminish Serbia and destroy her as a Balkan factor was, after all, the right method, even if he had succeeded in keeping the war "localized" and in temporarily strengthening the Dual Monarchy.

Supposing that Russia in 1914, because of military unpreparedness or lack of support, had been ready to tolerate the execution of Berchtold's designs, it is quite certain that she would have aimed within the next two or three years at wiping out this second humiliation, which was so much more damaging to her prestige than that of 1908–1909. In two or three years, when her great program of military reform was finally completed, Russia would certainly have found a pretext to reverse the balance in the Balkans in her own favor again. A further consequence of Berchtold's policy, even if successful, would have been the still closer consolidation of the Triple Entente, with the possible addition of Italy. And, finally, a partially dismembered Serbia would have become a still greater source of unrest and danger to the peace of Europe than heretofore. Serbian nationalism, like Polish nationalism, would have been intensified by partition. Austrian power and prestige would not have been so greatly increased as to be able to meet these new dangers. Berchtold's plan was a mere temporary improvement, but could not be a final solution of the Austro-Serbian antagonism. Franz Ferdinand and many others recognized this, and so long as he lived, no step in this fatal direction had been taken. It was the tragic fate of Austria that the only man who might have had the power and ability to develop Austria along sound lines became the innocent victim of the crime which was the occasion of the World War and so of her ultimate disruption.

Germany did not plot a European War, did not want one, and made genuine, though too belated efforts, to avert one. She was the victim of her alliance with Austria and of her own folly. Austria was her only dependable ally, Italy and Rumania having become nothing but allies in name. She could not throw her over, as otherwise she would stand isolated between Russia, where Pan-Slavism and armaments were growing stronger every year, and France, where Alsace-Lorraine, Delcassé's fall, and Agadir were not forgotten. Therefore, Bethmann felt bound to accede to Berchtold's request for support and gave him a free hand to deal with Serbia; he also hoped and expected to "localize" the Austro-Serbian conflict. Germany then gave grounds to the Entente for suspecting the sincerity of her peaceful intentions by her denial of any foreknowledge of the ultimatum, by her support and justification of it when it was published, and by her refusal of Sir Edward Grey's conference proposal. However, Germany by no means had Austria so completely under her thumb as the Entente Powers and many writers have assumed. It is true that Berchtold would hardly have embarked on his gambler's policy unless he had been assured that Germany would fulfill the obligations of the alliance, and to this extent Germany must share the great responsibility of Austria. But when Bethmann realized that Russia was likely to intervene, that England might not remain neutral, and that there was danger of a world war of which Germany and Austria would appear to be the instigators, he tried to call a halt on Austria, but it was too late. He pressed mediation proposals on Vienna, but Berchtold was insensible to the pressure, and the Entente Powers did not believe in the sincerity of his pressure, especially as they produced no results.

Germany's geographical position between France and Russia, and her inferiority in number of troops, had made necessary the plan of crushing the French army quickly at first and then turning against Russia. This was only possible, in the opinion of her strategists, by marching through Belgium, as it was generally anticipated by military men that she would do In case of a European War. On July 29, after Austria had declared war on Serbia, and after the Tsar had assented to general mobilization in Russia (though this was not known in Berlin and was later postponed for a day owing to the Kaiser's telegram to the Tsar), Bethmann took the precaution of sending to the German Minister In Brussels a sealed envelope. The Minister was not to open it except on further instructions. It contained the later demand for the passage of the German army through Belgium. This does not mean, however, that Germany had decided for war. In fact, Bethmann was one of the last of the statesmen to abandon hope of peace and to consent to the mobilization of his country's army. General mobilization of the continental armies took place in the following order: Serbia, Russia, Austria, France and Germany. General mobilization by a Great Power was commonly interpreted by military men in every country, though perhaps not by Sir Edward Grey, the Tsar, and some civilian officials, as meaning that the country was on the point of making war—that the military machine had begun to move and would not be stopped. Hence, when Germany learned of the Russian general mobilization, she sent ultimatums to St. Petersburg and Paris, warning that German mobilization would follow unless Russia suspended hers within twelve hours, and asking what would be the attitude of France. The answers being unsatisfactory,

Germany then mobilized and declared war. It was the hasty Russian general mobilization, assented to on July 29 and ordered on July 30, while Germany was still trying to bring Austria to accept mediation proposals, which finally rendered the European War inevitable.

Russia was partly responsible for the Austro-Serbian conflict because of the frequent encouragement which she had given at Belgrade—that Serbian national unity would be ultimately achieved with Russian assistance at Austrian expense. This had led the Belgrade Cabinet to hope for Russian support in case of a war with Austria, and the hope did not prove vain in July, 1914. Before this, to be sure, in the Bosnian Crisis and during the Balkan Wars, Russia had put restraint upon Serbia, because Russia, exhausted by the effects of the Russo-Japanese War, was not yet ready for a European struggle with the Teutonic Powers. But in 1914 her armaments, though not yet completed, had made such progress that the militarists were confident of success, if they had French and British support. In the spring of 1914, the Minister of War, Sukhomlinov, had published an article in a Russian newspaper, though without signing his name, to the effect, "Russia is ready, France must be ready also." Austria was convinced that Russia would ultimately aid Serbia, unless the Serbian danger were dealt with energetically after the Archduke's murder; she knew that Russia was growing stronger every year; but she doubted whether the Tsar's armaments had yet reached the point at which Russia would dare to intervene; she would therefore run less risk of Russian intervention and a European War if she used the Archduke's assassination as an excuse for weakening Serbia, than if she should postpone action until the future.

Russia's responsibility lay also in the secret preparatory military measures which she was making at the same time that she was carrying on diplomatic negotiations. These alarmed Germany and Austria. But it was primarily Russia's general mobilization, made when Germany was trying to bring Austria to a settlement, which precipitated the final catastrophe, causing Germany to mobilize and declare war.

The part of France is less clear than that of the other Great Powers, because she has not yet made a full publication of her documents. To be sure, M. Poincaré, in the fourth volume of his memoirs, has made a skillful and elaborate plea, to prove *La France innocente*. But he is not convincing. It is quite clear that on his visit to Russia he assured the Tsar's Government that France would support her as an ally in preventing Austria from humiliating or crushing Serbia. Paléologue renewed these assurances in a way to encourage Russia to take a strong hand. He did not attempt to restrain Russia from military measures which he knew would call forth German counter-measures and cause war. Nor did he keep his Government promptly and fully informed of the military steps which were being taken at St. Petersburg. President Poincaré, upon his return to France, made efforts for peace, but his great preoccupation was to minimize French and Russian preparatory measures and emphasize those of Germany, in order to secure the certainty of British support in a struggle which he now regarded as inevitable.

Sir Edward Grey made many sincere proposals for preserving peace; they all failed owing partly, but not exclusively, to Germany's attitude. Sir Edward could probably have prevented war if he had done either of two things. If, early in the crisis, he had acceded to the urging of France and Russia and given a strong warning to Germany that, in a European War, England would take the side of the Franco-Russian Alliance, this would probably have led Bethmann to exert an earlier and more effective pressure on Austria; and it would perhaps thereby have prevented the Austrian declaration of war on Serbia, and brought to a successful issue the "direct conversations" between Vienna and St. Petersburg. Or, if Sir Edward Grey had listened to German urging, and warned France and Russia early in the crisis, that if they became involved in war, England would remain neutral, probably Russia would have hesitated with her mobilizations, and France would probably have exerted a restraining influence at St. Petersburg. But Sir Edward Grey could not say that England would take the side of France and Russia, because he had a Cabinet nearly evenly divided, and he was not sure, early in the crisis, that public opinion in England would back him up in war against Germany. He could resign, and he says in his memoirs that he would have resigned, but that would have been no comfort or aid to France, who had come confidently to count upon British support. He was determined to say and do nothing which might encourage her with a hope which he could not fulfill. Therefore, in spite of the pleadings of the French, he refused to give them definite assurances until the probable German determination to go through Belgium made it clear that the Cabinet, and Parliament, and British public opinion would follow his lead in war on Germany. On the other hand, he was unwilling to heed the German pleadings that he exercise restraint at Paris and St. Petersburg, because he did not wish to endanger the Anglo-Russian Entente and the solidarity of the Triple Entente, because he felt a moral obligation to France, growing out of the Anglo-French military and naval conversations of the past years, and because he suspected that Germany was backing Austria up in an unjustifiable course and that Prussian militarists had taken the direction of affairs at Berlin out of the hands of Herr von Bethmann-Hollweg and the civilian authorities.

Italy exerted relatively little influence on the crisis in either direction. '

Belgium had done nothing in any way to justify the demand which Germany made upon her. With commendable prudence, at the very first news of the ominous Austrian ultimatum, she had foreseen the danger to which she might be exposed. She had accordingly instructed her representatives abroad as to the statements which they were to make in case Belgium should decide very suddenly to mobilize to protect her neutrality. On July 29, she placed her army upon "a strengthened war footing," but did not order complete mobilization until two days later, when Austria, Russia, and Germany had already done so, and war appeared inevitable. Even after being confronted with the terrible German ultimatum, at 7 p.m. on August 2, she did not at once invite the assistance of English and French troops to aid her in the defense of her soil and her neutrality against a certain German assault; it was not until German troops had actually violated her territory, on August 4, that she appealed for the assistance of the Powers which had guaranteed her neutrality. Belgium was the innocent victim of German strategic necessity. Though the German violation of Belgium was of enormous influence in forming public opinion as to the responsibility for the War after hostilities began, it was not a cause of the War, except insofar as it made it easier for Sir Edward Grey to bring England into it.

In the forty years following the Franco-Prussian War, as we have seen, there developed a system of alliances which divided Europe into two hostile groups. This hostility was accentuated by the increase of armaments, economic rivalry, nationalist ambitions and antagonisms, and newspaper incitement. But it is very doubtful whether all these dangerous tendencies would have actually led to war, had it not been for the assassination of Franz Ferdinand. That was the factor which consolidated the elements of hostility and started the rapid and complicated succession of events which culminated in a World War, and for that factor Serbian nationalism was primarily responsible.

But the verdict of the Versailles Treaty that Germany and her allies were responsible for the War, in view of the evidence now available, is historically unsound. It should therefore be revised. However, because of the popular feeling widespread in some of the Entente countries, it is doubtful whether a formal and legal revision is as yet practicable. There must first come a further revision by historical scholars, and through them of public opinion.

Harry Elmer Barnes
SUMMARY STATEMENT OF THE REVISIONIST POSITION

Like many Americans, Englishmen, and Frenchmen, Professor Barnes became convinced by the early publication of previously secret documents and memoirs that a great injustice had been done to Germany by Article 231 of the Versailles treaty. He left to other historians, however, the task of writing for scholars, and sought with noteworthy success to popularize the revisionist position. His presentation, based upon all the available sources, was the most forthright statement made by any student of the subject in the United States. More than any other work, it awakened a reaction in the minds and spirits of Americans to the wartime propaganda of condemnation and hatred of the enemy.

We have now devoted a series of chapters to the question of war responsibility in each of the major states involved. We may here briefly summarize the general situation in what may be regarded as a brief statement of the revisionist point of view as it appears to the present writer. The general European system after 1870, based as it was upon nationalism, militarism, secret alliances, and imperialistic aims, naturally inclined Europe toward war. The system does not, however, explain why war came in 1914, as the same general European situation had been prevailing for many years prior to that time, though certain problems had become more acute in the years immediately preceding the World War, particularly in the Near East and Morocco.

The Franco-Russian Alliance concluded by 1894 was transformed into an offensive organization following 1912 through the cooperation of Izvolski and Poincaré. Both recognized that the chief objects of Russian and French foreign policy, the seizure of the Straits and the return of Alsace-Lorraine, could be realized only through a general European war. From 1912–1914 their joint plans involved a manipulation of the Balkan situation in such a fashion as to be able to take advantage of any crisis likely to provoke a European war, an arrangement to get England so involved that she would be bound to come in on the side of France and Russia, and a great increase in military preparations in France and Russia.

It was decided that Serbia would be the most favorable area in which to create the desired incident in the Balkans. In the early spring of 1914 prominent officers in the Serbian General Staff laid a plot for the assassination of the Archduke, Franz Ferdinand. The Serbian civil government was aware of the plot for at least a month before its execution, but made no adequate effort to stop the plot or to warn Austria. Prominent Russians were also aware of the plot, but the degree of the complicity of Russia is as yet uncertain.

When the assassination came, the French and Russians recognized that the impending clash between Austria and Serbia would constitute a highly appropriate episode over which to bring about the desired conflict. The year 1914 was a particularly desirable year for the Entente because there was imminent danger that England might develop more happy relations with Germany, and that the French Radicals might be able to secure the repeal of the French Army Bill. Poincaré went to St. Petersburg, and, before knowing the terms of the Austrian ultimatum, renewed his pledge of two years earlier to support Russia in a war over the Balkans, and indicated that the probable Austro-Serbian conflict would meet the conditions demanded by the French in supporting Russia in intervention in the Balkans.

The Franco-Russian procedure in 1914 was to indicate a show of conciliation and concessions on the part of Serbia, and apparent Franco-Russian willingness to settle the dispute through diplomacy, while secret Franco-Russian military preparations were to be carried on which would ultimately make a diplomatic settlement quite impossible. Hence, Russia urged Serbia not to declare war on Austria, and, to insure a sufficiently conciliatory Serbian reply to Austria the Serbian response to the Austrian ultimatum was drafted in outline in the French Foreign Office. Russia did not desire to have Serbia precipitate matters prematurely by a declaration of war on Austria, because this would have affected European opinion, particularly English opinion, unfavorably and would also have brought about military activities altogether too rapidly for Russia, whose mobilization over a vast area would necessarily be slow as compared with that of Austria and Germany.

On the 24th of July, the moment Russia and France learned of the terms of the Austrian ultimatum to Serbia, they began that dual program of a diplomatic barrage combined with secret military preparations which had made a European war inevitable by the afternoon of July 30th. Russia sent a diplomatic message to Serbia counseling moderation, but at the same time decided upon the mobilization of the four great military districts of Central and Southern Russia as well as of the Russian fleets. Russian money in Germany and Austria was also called in.

On the same day Viviani telegraphed to the French Foreign Office that the Austro-Serbian situation was likely to develop serious European complications, and the French troops in Morocco were ordered home. Both countries began systematic military preparations for war on the 26th of July. By the 29th the time had come when Russian military preparations had gone far enough to warrant a general mobilization, and the Tsar was persuaded to consent to this order. A telegram from the Kaiser, however, induced him to revoke the order, but the next day Sazonoff and the army officials once more extracted from the Tsar his reluctant consent to the order for general mobilization. The French and the Russians had understood for a generation that once Russian general mobilization was ordered there would be no way of preventing a general European war. General Dobrorolski has told us with great candor that the Russian authorities in 1914 fully realized that a European war was *on* as soon as the mobilization order had been sent out of the general telegraph office in St. Petersburg late in the afternoon of July 30th.

The French authorities had been thoroughly informed as to the nature and progress of the Russian military preparations, but they made no effort to restrain them, though the French well knew that these military activities were bound to render a European war inevitable. They actually urged the Russians to speed up their military preparations, but to be more secretive about them, so as not to alienate England or provoke Germany to counter-mobilization. On the night of July 31st the French government went still further and finally decided for war, handing this information to Izvolski about midnight of the 31st. France was, thus, the first country to declare itself for war in the European crisis of 1914.

The Austrian statesmen in 1914 decided that the time had come when it would be necessary to control the Serbian menace, and they consciously planned an ultimatum to Serbia of such severity that it would be practically impossible for Serbia to concede all of these demands. The plan, then, was to make a show of diplomacy but to move toward certain war. This program was much like that of France and Russia, save for the fact that *Austria desired to provoke nothing but a local punitive war while the plans of France and Russia envisaged a general European conflict.* This is the most important point to be borne in mind when estimating the relative war guilt of Austria as against that of France and Russia.

Germany, formerly friendly to Serbia, was alarmed by the assassination of the Archduke and the resulting menace to her chief ally. Germany therefore agreed to stand behind Austria in the plan of the latter to execute her program of punishing Serbia. The answer of the Serbians to the Austrian ultimatum, however, impressed the Kaiser as satisfactory, and from that time on he was opposed to further military activity on the part of Austria against Serbia.

In cooperation with Sir Edward Grey, Germany began on the 27th of July to urge upon Austria direct negotiations with Russia and the mediation of her dispute with Serbia. Austria at first refused to listen to this advice and declared war upon Serbia on the 28th. Germany then became alarmed at the rumored Russian military preparations and vigorously pressed Austria for a diplomatic settlement of the dispute. Austria did not give way and consent to this until the 31st of

July, which was too late to avert a general European war because the Russian mobilization was then in full swing. Germany endeavored without success to secure the suspension of military activities by Russia, and then, after unexpected hesitation and deliberation, declared war upon Russia.

The Russian general mobilization, undertaken with full connivance of the French, was ordered at a time when diplomatic negotiations were moving rapidly toward a satisfactory settlement of the major problems in the crisis. Hence, the Russian general mobilization not only initiated military hostilities, but was also the sole reason for the failure of diplomatic efforts.

England was for peace provided France was not drawn into the conflict, but was determined to come into the War in case France was involved. As France decided from the beginning to stand with Russia for war, and as England refused to attempt to restrain either France or Russia, England was inevitably drawn away from her encouragement of the German efforts towards a diplomatic settlement of the crisis and into the support of the military aggression of France and Russia. She made her decision to enter the War after Germany had proposed to keep out of Belgium and to refrain from attacking France if England would remain neutral. In fact, Germany even suggested that she might guarantee the integrity of France and the French colonies in the event of war if England would promise neutrality. The Belgian issue in England was a pure subterfuge, exploited by Sir Edward Grey to inflame British opinion against Germany and to secure British support of his war policy.

The United States entered the War in part because the British blockade of the ports of the Central Powers led us to have our chief financial stake in the Entente, and partly because of the pro-British sympathies of Ambassador Page and President Wilson, which made it impossible for them to attempt to hold England strictly to international law on the seas. The English violations of international law in regard to neutral rights provoked the German submarine warfare in retaliation. This submarine warfare furnished the ostensible excuse for the American entry into the conflict. Yet, nearly a year before the resumption of submarine warfare, Mr. Wilson had secretly conveyed to England his intention to enter the war on the side of the Entente if Germany would not accept terms of peace which only a conquered state could have been expected to concede.

In estimating the order of guilt of the various countries we may safely say that the only direct and immediate responsibility for the World War falls upon Serbia, France and Russia, with the guilt about equally distributed. Next in order—far below France and Russia— would come Austria, though she never desired a general European war. Finally, we should place Germany and England as tied for last place, both being opposed to war in the 1914 crisis. Probably the German public was somewhat more favorable to military activities than the English people, but, as we have amply explained above, the Kaiser made much more strenuous efforts to preserve the peace of Europe in 1914 than did Sir Edward Grey.

George Peabody Gooch
RESPONSIBILITY OF POINCARÉ AND BETHMANN HOLLWEG

The dean of British historians early took an interest in the origins of the First World War, but in his published books he has not entered the war-guilt fray. His History of Modern Europe, 1878–1919 *(New York, 1923), exclusively devoted to international relations, was for many years the best available text on the period, but told the story as Gooch saw it without reference to the current controversy. With Harold Temperley, he supervised the selection and editing of the* British Documents on the Origins of the War, 1898–1914 *(London, 1926–1938, 11 v.). His books and articles have placed him in the camp of the revisionists, but his critical approach to his subject has marked him always as a thorough and unusually objective scholar rather than a special pleader. The first excerpt below is taken from his chapter on Poincaré. The second is from that on Bethmann Hollweg.*

Poincaré's stature was recognized in every quarter. He was never beloved, but the semi-official *Norddeutsche Allgemeine Zeitung* rightly saluted him as *l'homme de confiance* of the French people. "From the beginning of his Ministry he has been the living expres-

From G. P. Gooch, *Before the War*, II. *The Coming of the War* (London, New York, and Toronto, 1938), pp. 197–199, 284–286. Reprinted by permission of the publisher, Longman Group Ltd. Footnotes omitted.

sion of a great patriotic activity in the internal and external policy of his country. In the Eastern crisis he has put his talents at the service of European peace." In none of the extracts from the German press sent home by Jules Cambon is there a hint that he was regarded beyond the Rhine as a warmonger or an enemy. The dispatches of the Austrian Ambassador depict a statesman Russophil indeed, but far more moderate than Iswolsky. There is not a word in the five massive volumes of the *Documents diplomatiques français* covering his year at the Quai d'Orsay to suggest that he desired or worked for war. Not till the publication of selections from Iswolsky's dispatches in *Un Livre Noir*[1] in 1922 did the notion arise that in the closing months of 1912 he was recklessly playing with fire by giving Russia a free hand and indeed egging her on.

Poincaré's reply is that the Russian Ambassador, whom he distrusted and disliked, is a thoroughly unreliable witness. "In this jumble of documents published by the Bolshevists," he writes in his *Souvenirs,* "one can discover a few passages which, carefully separated from the context, are capable of different interpretations. But, as M. Herriot said in the Chamber of Deputies on July 6, 1922, if one studies the *Livre Noir* page by page, one finds nothing to compromise the Government of the Republic. . . . I knew that personal preoccupations played a capital part in his policy. Il ne se gênait pas pour substituer ses idées à celles de son gouvernement. Il traduisait à sa manière les instructions qu'il recevait et les réponses qui lui étaient faites au Quai d'Orsay. . . . Suivant une méthode chère à quelques représentants étrangers, il prêtait volontiers à ses interlocuteurs, dans sa correspondance officielle, le langage qu'il avait intérêt à leur faire tenir ou les conceptions qu'il voulait suggérer à son gouvernement, sans en prendre lui-même la responsabilité." ["He felt no constraint at substituting his own ideas for those of his government. He interpreted in his own way the instructions which he received and the replies which were made to him by the Quai d'Orsay. . . . Following a procedure favored by some foreign representatives, he, of his own volition, in his official correspondence attributed to those who talked with him the language which it was to his interest to have them use or the ideas which he wished to sug-

---

[1] A collection of Russian documents, translated by René Marchand from Soviet publications (2 v., Paris, 1922–1923).—Ed.

gest to his own government without having to take responsibility for them."]

Could Iswolsky have rebutted these grave accusations had he lived to read them? Probably not, though he would certainly have denied them. Not all diplomatists are equally accurate or conscientious reporters of conversations in which the turn of a phrase, the omission of a qualification, or the suppression of a point may make all the difference. Whatever may be thought of Poincaré's policy in 1912 or afterwards, his character stands higher than that of the Russian Ambassador. "I declare on my honor," he wrote shortly before his death, "that I never said a word to him which allowed him to expect from me an extension of the Franco-Russian alliance." Iswolsky's correspondence is an insufficient foundation for the graver charges leveled against him by critics at home and abroad. We approach nearest to the truth if we conclude that, like the ardent patriot he was, he put new vigor into French policy, and that, like a good lawyer, he operated the Russian alliance without straying beyond the letter of its obligations.

Yet the Russian Ambassador was correct in sensing an atmospheric change. Poincaré's accession to office, writes the most impartial and authoritative of French historians, opened a new phase, in which the French Government felt the need to revive the intimacy of the alliance. The experience of the Agadir crisis had shown what a bitter memory Russian statesmen retained of the attitude of France in the Bosnian crisis. If fresh Franco-German difficulties arose, was it not essential to count on stronger Russian support? And if reciprocity was to be assured, was it not necessay to manifest a greater interest in Russia's Balkan policy? That was the probable explanation of the new tendencies revealed in the application of the alliance in November 1912, when Poincaré, in view of a possible Austro-Russian conflict about a Serb port, adopted a more decided attitude. Of course he was very careful to say that the military support of France was limited to the *casus foederis,* that is to the hypothesis that Germany intervened to support Austria against Russia. But, unlike Pichon, he admitted the eventuality of a general war about Balkan questions.

In a word, under the stress of events, a broader interpretation of the partnership was advanced. The probability of a general conflict grew with the Agadir crisis and increased still further with the

Balkan struggle. The Grey-Cambon letters offered no such support as the logical French mind, which craves for precision, hungered to receive. Russia alone could be counted on in case of need, just as Germany and Austria formed an indivisible *bloc*. Bethmann's historic speech in the Reichstag on December 2, 1912, breathed the same message of unflinching solidarity as Poincaré's conversations with Iswolsky. Neither stateman had the slightest desire for a major conflagration, the result of which was unpredictable. Yet both were ready to fight for the Balance of Power, that master principle which inspired treaties, cemented ententes, and guided the Chancelleries of Europe on their perilous course.

Bethmann, like the other statesmen of 1914, never publicly acknowledged by tongue or pen any error of policy, but he was too conscientious to be entirely satisfied with himself. "When one comes to the question of responsibility for this war," he remarked to Theodor Wolff early in 1915, "we must candidly admit that we have our share of it. To say that I am oppressed by this thought would be to say too little. It never leaves me, I live in it. I am not speaking of this or the other diplomatic move which might perhaps have been made differently." Perhaps Bülow, he added, with his immense resourcefulness might have found his way out of the crisis.

The Hamlet of modern Germany, "The philosopher of Hohenfinow," as he was called, had inherited a situation which he was powerless to change. Like Grey he was a great gentleman and a sincere lover of peace; but he was an amateur in diplomacy and he was never master in his own house. He longed for the friendship of England, but he was forbidden to pay the price. With France there was nothing to be done. Italy was a member of the Triple Alliance only in name. The Potsdam agreement was a false dawn, for the incurable Austro-Russian rivalry remained. Thus, confronted by the Triple Entente, Germany was forced to lean ever more heavily on her only dependable ally, who naturally turned the altered relationship to account. Austria became the rider and Germany the horse. The paradox that the stronger Power should be taken in tow by the weaker was the result of the blunders which left Germany without other influential friends. When the testing time came in 1914 the policy of Berlin, as of Paris and London, was governed by the nightmare of isolation. Austria had determined to remove the Serbian menace. If she ceased to be a Great Power through the loss of her southern provinces Germany would stand alone, wedged in between a hostile Russia growing rapidly stronger and an irreconcilable France. From such a prospect even the mightiest of European states shrunk back in alarm. In the Bulgarian crisis of the eighties Bismarck had bluntly told his ally that he would not fight for her Balkan ambitions; but at that time the wire to St. Petersburg was working and he possessed the friendship of England, which his clumsy successors had lost. On the other hand he had declared in his apologia, in a passage which every German statesman knew by heart, that the maintenance of Austria as a Great Power was for Germany a condition of the European equilibrium for which the peace of the country might be sacrificed with an easy conscience in case of need.

When Francis Joseph inquired whether he might rely on the support of Germany, William II and his Chancellor answered that he could. A refusal would have devitalized if not actually destroyed the partnership of 1879. Moreover the Kaiser's appearance in shining armor at the side of the aged Emperor in 1909 had compelled Russia to keep the peace, and it was hoped that a fresh demonstration of solidarity might perhaps produce an equally satisfactory result. The mistake of Berlin was not in promising aid but in allowing Berchtold alone to steer the ship. In entering on such a perilous course, where the existence of the German nation was at stake, the Wilhelmstrasse should have insisted on consultation throughout. The decision whether there was to be a world war, declares Bethmann, lay with Russia, and the blame was hers. He failed to realize that she had no real choice. The situation had changed since the easy triumphs of the Bosnian crisis. If she lacked Austria's excuse of self-preservation, she was driven forward by peremptory considerations of prestige. She had recovered her strength and self-confidence. Serbia was flushed by her recent victories. England had drawn ever closer to her friends. The localization of an Austro-Serb conflict was too much to expect. Bethmann himself confesses his mistake in believing that Russia would shrink from the *ultima ratio,* and that England would prefer her friendship to the peace of the world. Warnings had reached him, but they were unheeded. Every war is a gamble, and the conflagration implicit in the German response to Austria's appeal was among the most desperate ventures in history. It is true that a struggle between the Teuton and the Slav was considered in Berlin to be almost inevitable; and, if it had to come, the German General Staff preferred 1914 to a later date, when Russia's strategic railways on the Polish front would be complete and the Three Years Service in France in full operation. Thus the civil and military authorities were ready for all eventualities if Russia intervened. Yet when all allowances are made for the difficulties of the situation and the inexperience of the Chancellor in the maze of foreign affairs, there is little excuse for stumbling into an undesired conflict when the best cards were in the hands of the foe. Whether Bülow or Tirpitz, his bitterest critics, would have done better is another question. It was a misfortune for the world that post-Bismarckian Germany produced no statesman of the first rank.

K. Zilliacus
ECONOMIC AND SOCIAL CAUSES OF THE WAR

Born in Kobe, Japan, of a Swedish-Finnish father and a Scotch-American mother, Konne Zilliacus went to school in Brooklyn, Finland, Sweden, and England, but returned to the United States to be graduated from Yale at the head of his class in 1915. After fighting in the First World War, he was a member of the Information Section of the League of Nations secretariat between the wars. During the Second World War he worked in the British Ministry of Information, and since 1945 has been a member of the House of Commons. His book, from which the following extract is taken, is subtitled A History of Secret Diplomacy, *and its message is that those who tackled reconstruction after 1919 failed because they tried to restore the prewar economic, social, and international conditions which had caused war in 1914.*

Why Britain Went to War

It is not necessary at this date to labor the point that this propaganda [that Britain went to war because Germany violated Belgian neutrality] was false in every particular, and that the governing class in Great Britain and every other belligerent country cared nothing

From *Mirror of the Past*, pp. 136–149. Copyright 1946 by K. Zilliacus, and published by A. A. Wyn, Inc., New York. All Rights Reserved. Reprinted by permission. Footnotes omitted.

at all for international law, or treaty obligations, or the rights of small nations. The *Times* was right when it wrote, on December 4, 1914, "We have always fought for the Balance of Power. We are fighting for it today."

Sir Arnold Wilson put the same point when he said in the House of Commons on February 24, 1936, in the course of a glowing tribute to Sir Edward (then Lord) Grey, that he would "go down in history as a man who was the foremost in keeping the bond of this country when he thought that the interests of the country required it."

This does not imply any lack of personal sincerity on the part of the Liberal government and the Foreign Office. They were intensely sincere in identifying their view of "national interests" with "honor" and "right." Nor was it more wrong for the Asquith-Grey government to play power politics in defense of imperialism than for any other great power to do the same.

But it does mean that there was a vast gulf between what the rulers of Great Britain were really fighting for and what they persuaded themselves and the British people that they were fighting for. The same discrepancy existed in all the belligerent countries. . . .

At this stage in our analysis of events it is sufficient to point out that whereas all the belligerents believed they were fighting in self-defense in a war that had been thrust upon them, each of them was in fact fighting a "preventive" war.

Austria-Hungary declared war on Serbia to prevent Pan-Serbian agitation from disrupting the Empire.

Russia mobilized against Austria to prevent Serbia from being crushed, for this would have meant Austro-German hegemony in the Balkans and Turkey and the end of Russian imperialist expansion in Southeast Europe and Asia Minor.

Germany backed Austria to prevent her from being crushed and Russian hegemony established in the Balkans, as that would have meant the end of German imperialist expansion in Southeast Europe and Asia Minor.

France supported Russia on the principle of "after Sadowa, Sedan"—i.e., if Germany won her war against Russia, she would become master of Central Europe from the Baltic to the Balkans, and would then be strong enough to help herself to French colonies.

Britain declared war on Germany because if Germany won her

war against France and Russia she would become master of all Europe, and strong enough to help herself to British colonies.

Each side was defending its imperialist interests by preventing the balance of power from being tipped in favor of its opponents. These imperialist interests were in the last analysis the private interests of finance and monopoly capital, which, through the influence of the plutocracy on governments and public opinion, were identified in the minds of the rulers with "national honor and vital interests." There were, of course, other factors in the situation, and the psychological process by which promoting vested interests in imperialism and war preparations is transmuted in men's minds into loyalty to religious, philanthropic, and patriotic ideals is complex and largely unconscious.

But the more closely world affairs before World War I are studied, the clearer it becomes that the pursuit of profits by finance capital was the chief "social dynamic" behind the drive for imperialism, protectionism,[1] and armaments. It was these vested interests that put up most of the money for Navy and Air and Empire leagues, Colonial Societies, and similar patriotic poisoners of public opinion. It was the plutocracy that owned part of the press and influenced most of the press through the control of advertising. It was the plutocracy that financed the British capitalist parties, whose leaders and members of Parliament were almost exclusively drawn from the class that lives by rent, interest, and profit.

These people did not believe in the rightness of what they were doing as much as they were unconscious of the possibility of doing differently. Their framework of experience was to them coincident with the limits of reality. Anything beyond was idle dreams or pernicious rubbish. They accepted the economic foundations of society as part of the order of nature, and the private profit-seeking motive as almost divinely inspired. Therefore the social dynamic of the drift to war operated below the threshold of their consciousness, in a sphere that they regarded as not subject to political control. It followed that their attitude to war was fatalistic. The idea that war was a man-made thing and that its causes could be ascertained

---

[1] Tariff wars played a big part in the growing tension between Germany and Russia and between Austria and Serbia. They were started and maintained for the usual mixed motives—power politics and vested interests.

and eliminated belonged, in their view, to the category of "idle dreams" and "pernicious rubbish." For to tackle the problem seriously meant disturbing the vested interests by which they lived and which to them seemed part of the order of nature.

Nothing is more striking in the story of how civilization collapsed in World War I than the sense of helplessness, of the governments and diplomats being mere puppets in the grip of blind forces. Mr. G. M. Trevelyan, in his *Lord Grey of Fallodon,* quotes the remark by Grey that "I used to hope that I was meant to keep the country out of war. But perhaps my real business was to bring her into it unitedly." It is not difficult to detect in this mystic resignation a refuge from the haunting sense of futility and failure.

As for the peoples, they were nothing at all, even in the most advanced democracies, except cannon fodder. No government ever dreamed of consulting them on matters of foreign policy, or hesitated to deceive them if they were presumptuous enough to question the ways of their rulers. All governments took it for granted that they would let themselves be butchered in unlimited quantities when the game of power politics made war necessary.

Conclusion

If even today public opinion learned the lesson of our failure to preserve peace in 1914, it might understand why we failed again in 1939. In that case we should have a better chance to win the peace after World War II than we did after World War I. For that lesson goes to the roots of the present situation, and if we profit by it we still have time to apply our hardly won wisdom to the new peace settlement.

It will take all the chapters of this book to reveal the full lesson. But let us endeavor to indicate the conclusions that would appear to emerge from what has been said hitherto. In doing so it will make things clearer to go from the particular to the general, beginning with specific criticisms of British foreign policy before 1914.

Let us take first the criticism that it was wrong for Great Britain to conclude the military and naval agreements. This is an argument for isolation. "Splendid isolation" was abandoned, as shown in the early part of this chapter, because Great Britain had ceased to be strong enough to defend the whole British Empire against all comers. And the British ruling class believed, and had persuaded public opinion to believe, that colonies were worth acquiring and keeping.

A variant of this view is that France and Great Britain should have remained neutral, and let Germany and Austria-Hungary defeat Russia. But in that case Germany would have become the master of all Central and Eastern Europe from the Baltic to the Balkans, and would have compelled France and Great Britain to surrender their colonial empires.

A Russian defeat, or a British refusal to lend the Czar the money to put down the first (1905) Russian Revolution, might, it is true, have resulted in a successful revolution in Russia that would have led to the democratization of Germany. But that would have meant a double risk. In the first place, it would have weakened the Entente temporarily in comparison with the central powers, and the latter might have exploited the situation to acquire a colony or two, or to push on in the Balkans. In the second place, once a revolution begins, one never knows how far it will go.

The governing class in pre-1914 days had not begun to be seriously disturbed about the stability of the social order. But at the back of their minds there was a little uneasiness that was now and again expressed in words. One catches glimpses from time to time of a social motive in foreign affairs. The previous chapter quoted Cecil Rhodes's view of imperialism as an antidote to social unrest. Lord Salisbury in the nineties complained:

> *Unfortunately we no longer live in the time of Pitt. Then the aristocracy was in power, and we could pursue an active policy which made England, after the Congress of Vienna, the richest and most respected of European Powers. Now the democracy rules, and has introduced a régime of persons and parties which has made every English Government dependent, unconditionally, on the* aura *popularis.... This generation can only be taught by events.*

The first treaty of the Triple Alliance, concluded in 1882, began with a preamble stating that the contracting parties had made this agreement in order "to increase the guarantees of general peace, to fortify the monarchical principle, and thereby to assure the unimpaired maintenance of the social and political order in their respective States."

The Kaiser, in commenting on the idea of disarmament in connection with the First Hague Conference (1899), objected that it would mean "handing over his towns to anarchy and democracy."

Isvolski, at the Second Hague Conference (1907), dismissed disarmament as "a dream of Jews, Socialists, and hysterical women."

At an early stage (July 23) of the negotiations during the fateful twelve days that swept the world into Armageddon, Sir Edward Grey warned the Austrian Ambassador that "if four great States, Austria-Hungary, Germany, Russia and France, should be involved in war," there would be economic bankruptcy and "the industrial centers in an uproar, so that in most countries, no matter who were victorious, many an existing institution would be swept away."

The Austrian Ambassador reports as follows his last talk with Sir Edward Grey, when all was lost and war was upon Britain:

> *Grey is in despair that his efforts to maintain the peace have gone to ruin. Again and again he said of the war, "I hate it, I hate it!" He recalled all the efforts we had made together, in the previous year, during the Balkan Conference. He had earnestly hoped that, once the present dangers were passed, it might be possible to preserve the peace for years. "I was quite ready if ever Russia had been aggressive—in the case of France it was not likely that she should—to stand by Germany, and that we might come to some sort of understanding between the Powers. Now all that was shattered, and universal war, with all its horrible and revolting consequences, had broken out.... It was the greatest step towards Socialism that could possibly have been made.... We should have Labour Governments in every country after this."*

This cry of the heart shows Sir Edward Grey's passionate sincerity about peace. But it also shows that the culminating horror of the world war to his mind was the danger of an advance towards socialism.

A Foreign Secretary who felt like that was not going to take any risk of encouraging revolution, either in Russia or anywhere else. He would prefer the certainty of power politics ultimately ending in a world war. And his feelings were not peculiar. They were typical of his Government, his diplomatic service, and his class.

A further criticism of British policy in those fatal three weeks was the failure to put pressure on Russia to postpone mobilization.

But Lowes Dickinson, who is inclined to agree with this criticism, points out that Russia had the assurance of French support and

> *would have risked war even without any certainty of British support. For consistently from the beginning she had made it clear that she would not stand by to see Serbia crushed by Austria. It is possible that Sir Edward was afraid that to stop Russia's preparations might encourage Germany to precipitate the war.*

The evidence adduced earlier in this chapter makes it clear that Russia, although the general staff finally forced the Czar's hand, did her best for some time to urge conciliation on Serbia and to secure a peaceful settlement, and that it was chiefly Germany and Austria that needed restraining—although the former did try to hold back Austria when she discovered—too late—that the British Government was going to stand by France. Bethmann-Hollweg says in his *Memoirs* that if he had only known earlier where Britain stood he could have restrained Austria and his own militarists and there would have been no war. In other words, if all concerned in Germany and Austria had known beforehand that they could not get away with a war, they might have kept the peace. Of the two, the Austrian Government, smarting under the assassination of the Archduke and really frightened of Pan-Serb propaganda, bore the chief, direct responsibility for turning the last diplomatic crisis into World War I.

There were occasions, notably during the Balkan Wars, when all the powers concerned had met in conference, when Sir Edward Grey helped to keep the peace by being careful, as Lowes Dickinson writes about the final crisis, "not to give the impression either that England would keep out of the war, under all circumstances, or that she would, necessarily, come in." But in 1914 this ambiguity, combined with the confusion and delays of diplomacy, played straight into the hands of those who pushed Europe over the edge.

On the other hand, there were two reasons why the British Government would not commit itself wholly to the Franco-Russian alliance. In the first place it was reluctant to give up the illusion of a free hand for the certainty of commitment, because it feared it would not get any corresponding measure of control over the foreign policies of the countries to which it was committed. Its members were genuine Liberals, in the sense of being reluctant and half-hearted about imperialism and power politics, and acquiescing in them only as the lesser evil (the greater evil being in their view the risks attaching to democracy in foreign politics).

In the second place, public opinion was isolationist and opposed to any commitments of any kind. Why, then, it may be asked, did not the Liberal government take the people into its confidence, and begin to educate them as to the necessity for an alliance to maintain the balance of power? Why did this course appear to it a greater evil than power politics and secret diplomacy?

The answer is that no one could tell where this process of democratizing foreign policy would stop. Many Liberals, and almost all Radicals and Labour men, were already displaying hostility to armaments and colonial imperialism. A certain Norman Angell had written an inconveniently plausible and popular book, in which he pointed out that the arguments of imperialists that colonies were necessary to the livelihood of the people were a "great illusion." Socialists had completed this demonstration by showing that the arms race and colonial buccaneering were inspired by the influence, of a more or less corrupt character, of big vested interests on governments and the press. It had not been altogether easy to keep public opinion from being too much interested in what was going on in Egypt, Morocco, Persia, and Tripoli. It would be optimistic to believe that the more the common people knew of these things, the readier they would be to pay in taxes, and finally in blood, for imperialism and power politics. For imperialism and power politics are the interest of plutocracy, but not of the common people. But the British Government saw no way of abandoning these things without shaking the foundations of the existing social order—that is, without incurring risks that were literally unthinkable.

To this day the British Foreign Office, unlike the rest of the civil service, is recruited by selection in addition to examination, and is the almost exclusive preserve of the upper middle class and the aristocracy. Before World War I this was wholly the case, and the Foreign Office was in complete charge of British foreign policy. Sir Edward Grey was little more than a dignified mouthpiece for his permanent officials. He had no policy of his own. He acted only as a sort of emollient and brake on their conduct of foreign policy, and as an intermediary between them and the few members of the Cabinet who were adjudged worthy to be let into the secret. . . .

In those days it was the governing class and the diplomats and military men who had a monopoly in the related domains of foreign affairs and defense. They were experts, who accepted unquestioningly the premises of imperialism and were skillful in playing the game of power politics that revolved about imperialism. They knew that public opinion was beginning to question the premises, and therefore tried to keep it ignorant of details, lest public opinion should learn too much and put an end to the whole game. . . .

The Foreign Office, by tradition, training, and class origin, saw "national interests" in terms of the interests of the plutocracy.

But let us not underestimate the difficulties of the Liberal government. It came into office in a world where international anarchy, power politics, and the arms race were the only known method of conducting international affairs, and where British imperialism was a going concern and faced by rival imperialisms. Liberals who might want to change these things knew they would have to fight the Foreign Office, the Colonial Office, and the fighting services, as well as the solidly imperialist and power-politics Conservative party.

Behind these hostile forces, and the press and propaganda they could command, were the plutocracy that subscribed most of the party funds to both the Liberal and Conservative parties. There was the difficulty that foreign powers would mistake concessions and conciliation for weakness, and merely ask for more. Although it was dangerous to educate public opinion out of its isolationism, it was difficult to innovate without the support of a militant and informed opinion. Liberals were impaled on the horns of an insoluble dilemma, and were borne along to World War I struggling vainly to free themselves.

The root of their difficulty and the fundamental fact that governed the situation were clearly stated as far back as 1903 by Mr. J. A. Hobson in his classic work, *Imperialism:*

> *It is not too much to say that the modern foreign policy of Great Britain is primarily a struggle for profitable markets of investment. To a larger extent every year Great Britain is becoming a nation living upon a tribute from abroad, and the classes who enjoy this tribute have an ever-increas-*

ing incentive to employ the public policy, the public purse, and the public force to extend the field of their private investments, and to safeguard and improve their existing investments. This is, perhaps, the most important fact in modern politics, and the obscurity in which it is wrapped constitutes the gravest danger to our State.

What is true of Great Britain is true likewise of France, Germany, the United States, and of all countries in which modern capitalism has placed large surplus savings in the hands of a plutocracy. . . . Thus we reach the conclusion that Imperialism is the endeavor of the great controllers of industry to broaden the channel for the flow of their surplus wealth by seeking foreign markets and foreign investments to take off the goods and capital they cannot sell or use at home.

There could be no solution of that difficulty so long as economic life was based on the private profit-seeking motive, which, magnified and concentrated through finance capital, exercised a decisive political influence without accepting any public control.

One school of German socialists did indeed invent the comforting doctrine of "ultra-imperialism." They believed that finance capital would tend to coalesce more and more across frontiers, into international trusts and combines that would lay the economic foundations for some form of world government based on the international exploitation of colonial territories. There were certain developments in this direction. But the main current ran strongly in the direction of more and more economic nationalism, imperialism, and war preparations.

The plutocracy, in short, showed no inclination to behave in the way German Social-Democrats had proved they must, and Norman Angellites argued they ought to, behave out of enlightened self-interest. They remained obstinately unenlightened, short-sighted, and selfish. Why this was, still is, and will probably remain the case until the plutocracy are literally put out of business need not be discussed at this juncture. It is enough to point out that this was so, and that the fact was of decisive importance in stultifying democracy and plunging the world into World War I.

*   *   *

If there is one lesson that stands out above all the others to be learned from the history of how World War I came, how the war ended, and what has happened since, it is the almost unbelievable blindness, tenacity, cruelty, and unscrupulousness with which the governing classes cling to their privileges and power at any cost to their suffering peoples and to the wider interests of peace and civilization. They are so expert and cunning on details, and so blind and foolish on fundamentals.

Pierre Renouvin
BACKGROUND OF THE WAR: GENERAL CONCLUSION

Professor of contemporary history and Dean of the Faculty of Letters at the Sorbonne, Professor of diplomatic history at the Institut d'Études Politiques, and member of the Institut de France, Pierre Renouvin stands at the peak of the historical profession in France. His major contribution to the controversy over war guilt, The Immediate Origins of the War, *appeared in English translation in 1928. Since then he has ranged widely over the fields of politics and diplomatic history, completing a seven-volume series on the history of international relations of which he has edited the earlier volumes and has himself written the last three on the period since 1815. Though he took an anti-revisionist position in his earlier works, he now presents the better balanced interpretation which emphasizes trends and movements rather than individual or national guilt; and while he recognizes economic and social forces he does not ascribe to them the importance that Zilliacus does.*

In surveying the whole of that period [1871–1914], which marked both the apogee of Europe and the first signs of its decline, diplomatic conflicts make sense only when considered within the framework of economic and social changes. The extension and accelerated tempo of industrial development; the rise of finance capitalism; the contrasts among social groups; the vast movements of transatlantic emigration; the spread of primary education; the power of the daily press; and also, not to be forgotten, the extension of military duties and obligations—all these aspects of a

From Pierre Renouvin, *Histoire des relations internationales:* VI. Le XIXe Siècle; 2e Partie: De 1871 à 1914 (Paris, 1955), pp. 377–84. By permission of Librairie Hachette. Editor's translation.

transformed world gave to international relations a new character. Consequently we must try to evaluate the respective influence of underlying causes and of diplomatic actions. . . .

With respect to the role of individual initiative, always important in diplomatic action, the "Bismarckian period" offers a contrast to the one that followed it.

How can one study the history of the period prior to 1890 without being struck by the deeds or the aims of that statesman toward whom all the others—Disraeli or Gladstone, Jules Ferry, Gorchakov —constantly looked? In the diplomatic correspondence nothing is more striking than the perpetual presence of the German chancellor or his shadow: What is Bismarck thinking and what is he getting ready to do? . . . "Bismarckism" is a reality of the collective psychology and consequently an indispensable explanatory element in the study of that epoch.

After the fall of the Chancellor the picture is quite altered. William II, failing to find "his Bismarck"—and even if he had met him, would he have supported him long?—was forced to push to the front of the stage some inferior actors, or at the very best a brilliant diplomat. Were the other European governments any better served? The epoch is poor in statesmen. On the one hand there is a disturbing levity, that of an Izvolski or a Berchtold, or a mediocrity that failed even to fool people at the time; on the other hand, there is the ordinary propriety of the high-ranking bureaucrat who disposes of the current business without ever looking beyond it; or, again, the confirmed parliamentarian who courts a "diplomatic success" even if this success is ineffectual or dangerous. Undoubtedly some men emerge from this grey monochrome because of striking characteristics: Salisbury's shrewdness and Raymond Poincaré's firmness of spirit, for example. But even among those whose work was most significant and whose program went beyond the customary horizon —Joseph Chamberlain, Delcassé, Aehrenthal—their strength of will and their audacity were more noteworthy than their farsightedness.

Around these ministers, what of those who collaborated with them in determining external policy?

The high diplomatic personnel in all the great states included many men whose professional conscientiousness, perspicacity in gathering political news, and dexterity in negotiation were excellent, and whose advice was taken. But nowhere, especially in France, did the great ambassadors during the twentieth century have enough character and personal authority to become, in grave situations, the counsellors of their governments, and to assume, even sometimes, the role of "mentors." Nowhere, moreover, did diplomatic agents exceed their instructions with more quiet assurance than in the Russian autocracy. The study of that diplomatic world remains indispensable for understanding its political practices, and without a doubt it allows us to catch a glimpse of a socially closed circle which in many cases tended to neglect profound changes and to believe that the aims or the maneuvers of chancelleries are the center of interest in international relations. But that very fact is one element in explaining the history of the time.

High military and naval personnel merit no less attention if we bear in mind the necessary harmony between the determination of external policy and the quality of the armed forces. Note that in the states whose regime was democratic and parliamentary the government, between 1900 and 1914, never stopped supervising the plans of the general staff, perhaps simply because it harbored a secret mistrust of military chiefs; and that, on the other hand, in Germany the general staff was freer in its action and freer to yield to the temptation to profit from a superiority in armaments.

It is nevertheless true that in the development of international "tensions," individual initiative at the beginning of the twentieth century was far from playing a role comparable with that which it had played between 1850 and 1870. One must look at Japan of the Meiji era and at the United States during Theodore Roosevelt's presidency in order to gain a different impression. On the "Old Continent" the actions of the statesman seemed to be dominated by conditions which perhaps he did not perceive clearly, and which he surely was incapable of mastering. Even in the final crisis when, however, certain "choices" taken by the governments seemed to be decisive, can one study these choices without taking account of the underlying forces?

It is therefore the influence of these forces which historical interpretation must try to evaluate.

The new place taken in the world by imperial Germany, the United States, and Japan at the end of the nineteenth and the beginning of the twentieth century is attributable in great part to the increase of population which supplied industry with labor and modified the ratios of military strength among the states. . . .

[But] the demographical situation became an essential factor only to the extent to which it was associated with the development of economic production, with financial power, and with a social structure capable of supplying officers for the armed forces. Russia, though it possessed almost half the population of Europe, was unable in that period to profit from this superiority because its industrial development had been slow, its public finances were at the mercy of foreign competition, and its supply of army officers was inadequate for lack of a sufficiently numerous middle class. . . .

The effect of economic and financial forces was manifested at every turn. It was directed above all by the influence of private interests and by the search for profits; but it also took national interests into consideration to the extent that citizens of the same state, despite the social conflicts that divided them, were conscious of their solidarity in relation to foreigners. These forces have been a powerful factor in the expansion of Europe toward other continents and, consequently, in the jealousies and rivalries which resulted from it, for the competition among the great European states in the conquest of new markets and reserves of raw materials, and for the "control" of land or sea communications has almost constantly weighed upon political relations. They had an essential role, even in Europe, in the development of the war potential and in the relative level of armed forces at the same time that they created between certain great states—especially Germany and England—mistrust and rancor. Germany, when it demanded its "place in the sun," was submitting to pressing economic necessities. This rise of economic power exercised, moreover, an influence on the national psychology or on the psychology of the social classes. In the sentiment of superiority, which has been held by the German people ever since the Bismarckian era and which began to be displayed in the United States at the end of the nineteenth century, the success gained in the industrial domain played a good part. Finally the attitude of a social group toward questions of external policy has sometimes been determined by economic and class interests.

All these facts corroborate the value of the "economic explanation" of history. But should one neglect the data that correct or limit it?

Rivalries between colonial imperialisms have often reached the critical point where the adversaries seemed to have said their "last word"; and yet these conflicts have not gone beyond threats: the Afghanistan question was regulated in 1885 by an Anglo-Russian compromise; the English cabinet, in spite of the importance of Far Eastern markets for the British economy, left Port Arthur to Russia in 1898; and the French government, as much as it wanted to reopen the "Egyptian question," recoiled at the time of Fashoda before the prospect of an armed conflict. Fundamentally governments and peoples have been conscious that these clashes over material interests were not worth a war, at least a "great war."

Competition between national economies does not seem to have been any more of a determinant. In the tension between France and Germany and in the German-Russian difficulties, economic interests have doubtless had a role, but a secondary one, as far as the present state of research makes it possible to judge. And in the "typical case," the Anglo-German commercial rivalry, what do we see? Did English business circles, even those most directly affected by German competition, dream of combating this competition by arms? There is no evidence that would let us think so; and the state of mind of the financiers in the City, hostile in 1914 to an armed intervention on the Continent, dictates a negative answer. Did the great German industrialists, in order to avoid possible but future dangers, have an interest in making war on Russia, their best European supplier, and on Great Britain, their best customer? Did they need to open up by force of arms any new foreign markets, when the prosperity of their enterprises in 1914 was in no way menaced for the immediate future, and when the perspective had been opened to them of enlarging their outlets in Asia Minor and in Africa by agreements concluded with Great Britain? It must be said that proofs are lacking....

But the vigorous assertion of national feeling is one of the basic traits of the period. There were the protests of "national minorities," subjected to a foreign domination, on the one hand, and, on the other, the growth of nationalisms which did not shrink from invoking the security interests of the state and appealing to traditions or permanent principles, often doubtful or illusory, but which expressed the desire for prestige and the will to power. The nationalistic movement shook the Balkan peninsula, threatened the existence of Austria-Hungary, disturbed Russia and Great Britain. Nationalism asserted itself in the majority of great European states, while it lay at the root of the new Japanese power; national sentiment was finally awakened even in China when European pressure there became too heavy.

In many cases this force took into its service the economic or financial interests which became the instruments of political action instead of being the driving power behind it; tariff and capital investments policies were often adopted by the state for the sake of its desire for power.

Historical explanation cannot be more simple than the behavior of human groups. If it isolates one of the aspects of this behavior, it falsifies it because, between the attraction of material interests and the impulsion of nationalist feelings, the influences are reciprocal. In 1914 the relations among the states would have looked quite different if the economic life of the world had not undergone some profound changes in the course of the preceding half century. But does that mean that the European war was the necessary result of the clash between material interests? In fact, the conflict occurred only at the moment when political considerations—concern for safeguarding security or the desire for power—clashed violently. Without doubt, in these same considerations economic interests might have had a place, for governments and people did not ignore the material advantages that success would bring them. But it was not this calculation that guided their acquiescence or their choice of action. The effective impulsion came from national feeling and from passionate emotions.

Raymond Aron
CAUSES AND RESPONSIBILITIES

*Able editorial writer for the well-known Paris newspaper, Le Figaro, and
Professor at the Sorbonne and the Institut d'Études Politiques, Raymond
Aron is concerned with the analysis of "total war" as it has developed in the
twentieth century. His discussion of the origins of the First World War serves
both as an introduction to the main body of his study and as a means of
pointing out that public opinion is a new element in modern wars. He, like
Renouvin, emphasizes tensions and national interests. His treatment of the
problem represents the detached and scholarly approach that had succeeded the emotional involvement of the early war-guilt literature.*

Frederick the Great left to his legal apologists the justification of
his conquests after they had taken place. Public opinion played
hardly any part in the limited warfare of the eighteenth century; the
professional soldiers, recruited from the lower classes of society,
felt no need to know why they were fighting. In the twentieth century, the soldier and citizen have become interchangeable; and the
general public, believing itself peacefully disposed, demands an
accounting from its leaders. To prove the enemy responsible for a
war has become each government's duty. On each side, historians
and intellectuals strive not so much to maintain the morale of the
fighting forces alone as to clear the conscience of the whole nation.

The analysis of the origins of the First World War, originally based
upon the need for propaganda between 1914 and 1918, was carried
on, even after the Allied victory, by a sort of revolt against what had
happened. Middle-class Europe, proud of its civilization and sure of
its progressiveness, regarded war as a monstrosity out of another
age. The authors of the Treaty of Versailles demanded reparations,
invoking not the defeat in arms, which the vanquished Germans
(well aware of what they themselves would have done had they
been victorious) would have accepted without demur, but the fact of
aggression. The study of the causes of the war was inspired not as
much by historical curiosity as by that spirit of moral righteousness.
Who were the criminals who had plunged Europe into the abyss of

violence? What fortuitous elements had revived the horrors of the past?

Historical research yielded inconclusive results. It did not make an end of uncertainties. Inevitably it disappointed both the pacifists and those who sat in judgment.

The historian, concerned to show the causes of an event, puts two questions, both legitimate, but which must be carefully distinguished. First of all, why did war come at that particular time; and, given the situation, who were the men, or what were the circumstances, that precipitated war? Secondly, how was the situation which led to the war created? The first question refers to what are generally called the immediate causes, the second to what are called the remote origins. Historians attribute to the former more or less importance according to their philosophy and also to the results of their inquiry. If they come to the conclusion that the situation led inevitably to war, the immediate causes obviously lost importance.

In their study of the First World War, historians were deeply interested in the immediate causes. The actual events marshaled themselves in a highly orderly fashion. Before the assassination of the Archduke Francis Ferdinand, Europe was living in a state of preparedness, but no one expected an outbreak from one day to the next. Following the assassination, and especially after the Austrian ultimatum to Serbia, chancelleries and populations alike felt the dread of approaching disaster.

A multitude of books and commentaries have attempted to explain the week that passed between July 23, when Austria dispatched her ultimatum to Serbia, and the thirtieth, the day on which Russian mobilization was decreed. Archives have been exhausted, responsible leaders have published their memoirs, and historians have reconstituted the conversations, negotiations, and interviews that had taken place in Vienna, Berlin, St. Petersburg, and Paris. The very accumulation of documents seemed to result in confusion.

More apparent than real, the confusion is based upon three interrelated questions: What were the actions that rendered war not only possible, but probable, and finally inevitable? Up to what point were those actions morally or politically legitimate? What were the intentions of those responsible for them?

No one denies today, as no one doubted then, that the Austrian ultimatum introduced the possibility not only of war, but of general war. The statesmen at Vienna were aware of that risk, just as the German statesmen had recognized it at the discussions in Berlin at the beginning of July. Russia, who regarded herself as protectress of the European Slavs in the Balkans, would not allow Serbia to be crushed or permit her to be transformed from an independent kingdom into a sort of protectorate of the Dual Monarchy. The ultimatum was a challenge to Russia. All Europe realized that the initiative, heavy with menace, had come from Vienna, and that it would not have been taken without the promise of support given in Berlin.

The Serbian reply was moderate in its terms, though it rejected the proposal that Austrian officials participate in an inquiry. If we add to the ultimatum the refusal to accept Serbia's reply, and then the severance of diplomatic relations and the bombardment of Belgrade, we have a succession of acts for which Austrian diplomacy (and indirectly German diplomacy) may be held responsible. This, then, was the European situation in 1914 which made likely the advent of a general war.

Controversy has centered mainly on the legitimacy of the Austrian policy. To what extent did the conduct of the Serbian Government justify what were exorbitant demands under international law? Whatever particular Serbian officials or private politicians might have had to do with the preparation of the Archduke's assassination, the facts known at the time gave no ground for holding the Belgrade Government responsible, and consequently gave the Vienna Government no authority to make demands incompatible with Serbian sovereignty. For the rest, there is little doubt that the Austrian diplomats neither desired nor expected a simple acceptance of their ultimatum. They wanted to "teach a lesson" to the little country that was disturbing its powerful neighbor by supporting or tolerating the "liberation" propaganda of the European Slavs. The men who had determined at Vienna to "teach the lesson" resolutely accepted the possible consequences, including general war.

Thus the real issue is whether we may consider these consequences to have been possible, probable, or inevitable. There is little likelihood of a unanimous conclusion. The historian may ponder the influence of one event on another but his conclusions can never be final. In the present case, one must at least say that the Central Powers had created conditions which rendered war probable.

Would its avoidance have required a miracle, or merely more diplomatic patience and imagination in the opposite camp? Speculations on what *might* have happened are endless.

The same sort of controversy was carried on over the Russian general mobilization, the first in date (though, before it became known, the Austrian mobilization had been decided on). Was not that mobilization politically legitimate as a reply to the first operations against Serbia? The German military leaders themselves regarded the Russian mobilization as different in nature from all the other ones because of the time that it required. When that mobilization took place, had not the die been cast, and were not the general staffs in the different capitals impatient to set going a mechanism which left diplomacy no further room for action?

As long as we consider only the two questions of causality and legitimacy, careful inquiry compels us to qualify, but without fundamentally modifying, the Allied contention. It was the Vienna Cabinet that took the initiatives which all Europe has held to be bellicose. It was that Cabinet which threw down the glove to Serbia, and therefore to Russia; it was that Cabinet which wanted a *succès de prestige,* even at the risk of general war. Germany, in giving Vienna a free hand, shared the responsibility, whatever may have been the secret thoughts of her rulers. Even though it were shown that the Entente, and Russia in particular, was too prompt in taking up the challenge, the burden of guilt in the diplomatic sequence of actions and rejoinders would remain with the "initiators."

But such guilt, positive and limited—diplomatic, so to speak—is incommensurable with that imagined by popular passion. Search was made, not for this or that Minister bent on extirpating the Irredentist propaganda of the European Slavs, but for the men who had knowingly embarked on aggression. They were not discovered or, in any case, they were not discovered in the simple guise of storybook villains.

The search for motives or incentives leads to unending controversies. It is possible on the basis of certain testimony to represent German policy as inspired by the desire to launch as soon as possible a war considered to be inevitable. The proposals of Wilhelm II to the King of the Belgians may be adduced, for example. In certain military quarters it was obviously thought that the reorganization of the Russian Army would not be completed until 1917, and that the

French forces were short of machine guns and heavy artillery. Such considerations, reinforcing the confidence of the general staff, must have influenced the generals in the discussions at the beginning of July. But the study of archives has revealed a German policy less sure of itself and less definite in its aim. Berlin accepted general war, but it could not be said that the responsible statesmen deliberately set out to provoke it over the Austro-Serbian dispute. That idea certainly crossed the minds of some persons at some moments, but it did not constantly determine the action of the Chancellor, the Emperor, or the Ambassadors.

In other words, when we search for motives the simple picture of aggressors and victims does not stand up to rigorous analysis.

The French statesmen certainly desired war even less. The Tsar and a good many (but not all) of the Russian leaders were afraid of war, perhaps more out of concern for the regime than for the war itself. But the Allies were determined not to tolerate the Austrians' resorting to force in the Balkans, while Viennese diplomacy was no less determined to use force if necessary to gain a *succès de prestige* at the expense of Serbia. On both sides the will to peace was conditional, not absolute. The European situation in 1914 made the localization of the conflict extremely improbable, but both Berlin and Vienna would have been satisfied to attain the immediate objective without starting a general war.

The European scene was not occupied by "sheep and wolf" states, but by sovereign states equally determined to maintain their power and prestige. In Britain and France there was no equivalent of the Pan-Germans or the romantic theorists of violence. Both countries were inclined to be conservative and to renounce dreams of conquest. The Germany of Wilhelm II, actively expansionist, was more inclined to the call of arms than the middle-class democracies. For all that, the explosion in 1914 was the result of diplomatic failure.

For a century Europe had enjoyed relative stability. Neither the Crimean War nor the Franco-Prussian War became general. With greater effort the Balkan Wars were brought to an end without irreparable injury to the European equilibrium. The "war monster" that had shaken the Continent from 1792 to 1815 had been chained up. It broke loose again in August 1914.

As soon as we leave the narrow limits of our inquiry into the assassination of the Archduke and the Austrian declaration of war, going back before the crisis of June and July 1914, there is no longer any date that can be regarded as marking the origin of the historical situation that produced the First World War. The Franco-German hostility leads us back at least to the Treaty of Frankfurt, the Russo-German hostility at least to the abandonment of the Re-insurance Treaty by the young Emperor Wilhelm II. But rather than retrace a half century of European diplomatic history, our critical inquiry must restrict itself to the formulation of definite questions.

Any student of the crisis was bound to be struck by the rapidity with which an incident involving an individual prince set all Europe ablaze. Why had the situation become so explosive? Why did so many statesmen and common men alike vaguely sense the rising storm?

The replies of the historians, although differing in detail, are on the whole irresistibly simple, disconcerting to those who want to penetrate beyond the superficial facts and root out the deep-seated forces of which the very participants themselves had no knowledge.

In accordance with an unwritten law of European diplomacy, the very fact of Germany's growth in power provoked a grouping of nations to make a stand against her. The course of the war proved abundantly that the Triple Entente had no surplus of strength over the German-Austrian alliance. But the fact that the Entente was necessary for equilibrium does not explain why it was formed. It had not yet been formed at the end of the last century, though the same considerations had already made it necessary. We must there-fore remember simply that the grouping of the great European na-tions into more or less close alliances was something neither novel nor monstrous that required a special explanation or implied the existence of a culprit.

France, once she had surmounted the consequences of defeat, would normally, in accordance with an old tradition, seek support in the East. It may be that the Franco-Russian rapprochement was facilitated or accelerated by the mistakes of the Wilhelmstrasse. But it would have been difficult, in the long run, for Germany to remain very friendly with both Russia and Austria-Hungary. In pre-ferring the latter she inevitably brought about a rapprochement be-tween Paris and St. Petersburg. As for Great Britain, she was bound to fear a German victory that would eliminate France as a major power and give the conqueror almost unlimited hegemony over the Continent. British diplomacy would perhaps not have heeded the peril to its own profound interests had not the Second Reich, by building a military fleet, delivered a challenge which the British Empire could not refuse.

For the rest, from the beginning of the century there was a lack of definition in the diplomatic "fronts." Contacts between the courts of Berlin and St. Petersburg were frequent until the eve of the rupture. Wilhelm II tried several times to take advantage of his personal ascendancy over Nicholas II for purposes of high diplomacy. The treaty signed by the two Emperors at Björkö in July 1905, although subsequently rejected by the Tsar's Ministers, must not be forgotten. Until the eve of the catastrophe the relations between London and Berlin, quite apart from dynastic ties, were not those of irreconcilable enemies. As late as 1914 British Ministers had the idea of appeasing German ambitions by negotiating a partition of the Portuguese colonies. In spite of the efforts of French diplomacy, no British Government had entered into any formal engagement: discussions between the general staffs did not interfere with the freedom of decision of the London Cabinet.

The division of the principal nations of Europe into two camps did not necessarily make for war. It only made it inevitable that any conflict involving two great powers would bring general war. From the moment when there was formed in the center of Europe a German empire, industrially foremost in Europe, with a population exceeding that of France by more than 50 percent, and allied to the Dual Monarchy, a war on the small scale of that of 1870 had become impossible. Neither Russia nor Great Britain would have tolerated a new German victory which would have made of the Reich no longer merely the dominant European state, but a claimant to empire over the Continent.

The two camps were not condemned to mortal combat by any mysterious fatality. The relations between the coalitions had simply deteriorated until clear-sighted observers foresaw the inescapable outcome of armed peace. Who was to blame? The issue has been passionately argued. One side denounced the intolerable manners of Teutonic diplomacy, the demand for Delcassé's dismissal, the spectacular visit to Tangier, the dispatch of a gunboat to Agadir, the annexation of Bosnia-Herzegovina; on the other side it was pointed out that in the course of the half century during which she had been the foremost power on the Continent, Germany had added less to her overseas possessions and profited less by arms or negotiation than weakened France. Germany had made herself intolerable by her brutality, by her arrogance, and by the ambitions of which she was suspected. But under the rules of diplomacy she was not wrong in demanding compensation when France established her protectorate over Morocco. She could not fail to notice that the international conferences were not turning out to her advantage.

The growing tension centered about three principal difficulties: the rivalry between Austria and Russia in the Balkans, the Franco-German conflict over Morocco, and the arms race—on sea between Britain and Germany, and on land between all the powers. The two last causes had produced the situation, the first one kindled the spark.

There are doubtless those who contend that the immediate cause matters little, and that war might have broken out just as easily in 1911 as in 1914. The contention readily suggests itself and is not easily disproven. The fact remains that the Balkan quarrels brought about the actual rupture, just as they had helped to dissolve the pact of conservation which, despite divergent alliances, still united the sovereigns of Russia and Germany. For one thing, the clash between Russia and Austria-Hungary had a diplomatic cause. Repulsed in Asia after her defeat by Japan in 1905, Russia conformed to tradition and redirected her attention and her ambitions to Europe. But, apart from diplomacy, the clash had a deeper cause in the movement of ideas and passions. For two supranational empires still existed in an age of nationalism. The Ottoman Empire had not yet been liquidated, and already diplomats were anxiously anticipating the time when they would have to face the problem of the succession to Austria-Hungary.

Henceforth Viennese diplomacy is more understandable. It was no longer so much a question of avenging the assassination of an Archduke who had favored trialism and whose disappearance pleased many persons in high places. It was a matter of ending once and for all the nationalist propaganda that challenged the existence of Austria-Hungary. Obviously, Russia could not allow the Vienna Government a free hand.

The quarrel between chancelleries interested also the general public in each country. Diplomacy had succeeded in integrating into the Europe which followed the Congress of Vienna a united Germany and a united Italy without a general war. It was unable to perform such a feat again in the twentieth century. The national conflicts in Eastern Europe unleashed a general war.

The inquiry into political responsibility carries with it no authority to banish as criminals either men or nations. But inquiry does clarify the significance and the origins of the war. The immediate occasion and the deeper cause largely coincide; for, as we have seen, the reasons for hostility among the various nations of Europe were manifold. The relative strengths and the relationships of alliance excluded partial conflicts. The rise of Germany, whose hegemony France dreaded and whose navy menaced England, had created an opposition that claimed to be defensive but was denounced by German propaganda as an attempt at encirclement. The two camps alarmed each other, and each tried to soothe its own fears by piling up defensive armaments. The atmosphere grew heavy with multiplied incidents, which spread the conviction of approaching disaster. The explosion finally came in the East, where Russia and Austria were advancing contradictory claims, and where the principle of national sovereignty had ruined the Ottoman Empire and was beginning to undermine the still imposing edifice of the Austro-Hungarian Empire.

II THE GERMAN WAR-GUILT QUESTION REVIVED

Fritz Fischer
GERMANY AND THE OUTBREAK OF WAR

Professor of History at Hamburg University, Fischer's main concern in his book, Germany's Aims in the First World War, *is to show that Germany was pursuing an aggressive policy, inspired by economic interests and designed to achieve world power. He begins with a chapter on German policy from about 1900 to 1914, then in chapter 2, reprinted below, he examines the July crisis of 1914 before launching into the aims of the war period. In his view there is a continuity in German objectives from 1900 to the Second World War, although the link between the first and second wars is implied rather than spelled out. The English-language text was reduced by the author himself by about a third from the third edition of the German work. As Imanuel Geiss, one of his students, has pointed out, Fischer not only questioned the taboo of German innocence, built up in Germany over five decades, but also broke the monopoly of knowledge that conservative German historians had held by "just picking up Albertini and reading the documents published since 1919." Furthermore his book helped to divert attention from purely diplomatic to economic considerations.*

In spite of all the surface calm, the feeling, or conviction, that a great European conflict could not be long postponed had become general in Europe. Germany found herself, as Moltke put it, "in a condition of hopeless isolation which was growing ever more hopeless." Her confidence in the invincibility of her military strength had been deeply shaken by the increases in the French and Russian armies (of which the latter would in 1917 reach its maximum peacetime strength of 2 million men), and the idea of a "preventive war" was acquiring an increasing appeal, especially in military circles. "We are ready, and the sooner it comes, the better for us," said Moltke on June 1, 1914. At about the same time, Moltke asked Jagow to precipitate a preventive war as soon as possible. Jagow refused, but admitted later that he had never wholly excluded the idea of a preventive war and that Moltke's words had influenced him during the crisis of July–August 1914. Another element of danger was the fact that Conservative circles had come, especially since the Reichstag elections of 1912, to regard war as a "tempering of the nation" and calculated to strengthen the Prusso-German state. Bethmann Hollweg, who in December, 1913, had already rejected the suggestion passed on to him by the crown prince, and emanating from the pan-Germans, that a coup d'état should be carried out against the Social Democrats, spoke out again just six months later against these speculations on the internal political consequences of a war. He told Lerchenfeld, the Bavarian minister, at the beginning of June, 1914, that:

> *There were still circles in the Reich which looked to war to bring about an improvement, in the conservative sense, of internal conditions in Germany. He thought that the effects would be the exact opposite; a world war, with its incalculable consequences, would greatly increase the power of Social Democracy, because it had preached peace, and would bring down many a throne.*

A month later the Chancellor agreed on foreign-political and military grounds to take the risk of a great war, while recognizing—unlike the Conservatives—that the war could not be carried on without the cooperation of Social Democracy.

Sarajevo, the Hoyos Mission and Germany's Blank Check

The news of the murder of the heir to the Austro-Hungarian throne evoked indignation and consternation throughout Europe, but there was no feeling that it must inevitably lead to a European crisis. The reactions were mixed in the Monarchy itself. There was genuine mourning; but a close observer could not fail to note that wide circles in the Monarchy felt undisguised relief at the death of the man who meant to put through some sort of trialist or federalist reorganization of the Monarchy favorable to its Slavonic elements. Besides the Germans and Magyars, who had felt their dominating positions threatened by Franz Ferdinand, and besides the Emperor Franz Joseph, who had never forgiven his nephew his morganatic marriage, there was also a third group in the Monarchy who welcomed the archduke's death, because they saw in it an opportunity to settle accounts once and for all with Serbia by a war in which Germany would be behind them. The spokesman of this group was Baron Conrad von Hötzendorf, Chief of the Austro-Hungarian General Staff. Although since 1912 Conrad had described the idea of a military reckoning with Serbia as a *va banque* gamble, if it had to be risked without the support of Rumania—on which he had counted confidently in 1905—and with a stronger Russia, only a few days after the murder he thought that the conflict with Serbia, bad as its prospects were, could no longer be avoided, and immediately the news reached him he told the Austro-Hungarian Foreign Minister, Berchtold, that Austria should mobilize; she should "cut through the knot," or her prestige would be gone forever and her position among the great powers be irretrievably lost. But even this thruster, when he tried to persuade the hesitant diplomats, Berchtold and his assistant, Forgach, to adopt the military solution, was not willing to risk war without a firm promise of help from Germany. The Emperor was for taking the risk. Tisza, the Hungarian Prime Minister, was more doubtful than Berchtold himself; the political situation was unfavorable, Russia too strong, public opinion unprepared. The final decision thus depended on Germany's attitude. Both the German ambassador in Vienna, von Tschirschky, and Zimmermann, the Under-Secretary of State in the Foreign Ministry (Jagow, his chief, was away on his honeymoon), were at first very reserved and counseled moderation.

But this policy of hesitancy was abruptly altered by Wilhelm II, who was outraged that the ambassador should take so much upon himself. By July 4 the Emperor was all for "settling accounts with Serbia." "Tschirschky will be so good as to drop this nonsense. We must finish with the Serbs, *quickly*." With his famous words "now or never" the Emperor laid down the general course of Germany's policy for the next weeks. From that hour Tschirschky and Zimmermann were among the most decided advocates of a hard policy towards Serbia.

This reversal of attitude came as no surprise to Austria-Hungary. On July 1 the German publicist Victor Naumann, a confidant of the German Foreign Ministry, had been in Vienna and had talked to Count Hoyos, the permanent head of the Austro-Hungarian Foreign Ministry, to whom he had given an illuminating sketch of the mentality then prevailing in leading political circles of Germany. The conversation was afterwards officially described as having been purely private; what made it so important was that Germany's actual behavior in the July crisis exactly confirmed Naumann's prophecies. The heads of the services thought the Triple Alliance "not strong

enough at present," but the adherents of the idea of a preventive
war were growing steadily, both in the army and navy, and in the
Foreign Ministry. This "idea" was also supported by a second consideration. It was hoped that the Anglo-German settlement in Africa
had "made it certain that Britain would not intervene in a European
war." Naumann openly counseled military action against Serbia. The
Triple Alliance was strong, Britain would be neutral. The Foreign
Ministry, as he knew from von Stumm, would certainly not oppose
it, and—the fourth favorable factor—the Emperor would not shrink
from war, as he had in the Moroccan crises. Moreover, public opinion would force the Foreign Ministry to let things take their course.

On July 4 the Austrian Foreign Ministry had been unofficially informed by Tschirschky, through an *homme de confiance* of the German embassy, that "Germany would support the Monarchy through
thick and thin, whatever action it decided to take against Serbia. The
sooner Austria-Hungary struck, the better."

Since Conrad's plans for war against Serbia were dependent on
Germany's support, the first essential for Vienna was to secure official information on Germany's definitive intentions. Count Hoyos was
sent to Berlin to obtain this. On July 5 he handed Szögyény, the
Austro-Hungarian ambassador in Berlin, two documents: a memorandum, compiled by Tisza, on the situation of the Monarchy, cou-
pled with a proposal that advantage should be taken of the Serbian
question to attach Bulgaria to the Triple Alliance, and a letter in
Franz Joseph's own hand to the effect that the only way of saving
the Monarchy from being swallowed up in the "Pan-Slav flood" was
"to eliminate Serbia, which at present constitutes the corner-stone
of pan-Slav policy," as a political power-factor in the Balkans.
Szögyény handed the two documents to the Emperor the same day.
At first the Emperor evaded taking a decision, but after lunch, to
which he had invited Szögyény in the Neues Palais in Potsdam, he
authorized him to inform his monarch that Austria-Hungary could
"count on Germany's full support" even in the case of "grave European complications"; Germany, "loyal as ever to her ally," would
stand by Austria even should the Serbian conflict lead to war between Austria and Russia. Wilhelm even told the ambassador that if
Vienna should decide on military action against Serbia, she ought
to march at once. He thought that he could himself dispel Austria's
anxieties about Rumania's attitude by a personal intervention with

King Carol. At the same time he told Szögyény what had been the chief consideration that had made it so easy for him to decide to support Austria-Hungary: "In any case, as things stood today, Russia was not at all ready for war, and would certainly think long before appealing to arms."

This was, as we shall see, one of the basic assumptions of German policy in these weeks: that Russia and France were still militarily weak enough to enable Germany to weather the crisis, however it developed.

When the audience was over, Szögyény was able on the same day to pass this "blank check" of the German Emperor to Vienna, and to report that Wilhelm II "would regret it if we (Austria-Hungary) let this present chance, which was so favorable for us, go by without utilizing it." The Emperor had indeed made the reservation, which the constitution imposed on him, that he must get the Imperial Chancellor's consent, but he had had no doubt, as he had expressly emphasized, that Bethmann Hollweg "would entirely agree with him."

This was exactly what happened. Bethmann Hollweg and Zimmermann were summoned to Potsdam the same afternoon, and to them the Emperor unfolded the same train of thought he had to Szögyény; and, as Wilhelm expected, Bethmann Hollweg, who did not yet know the exact text of the Austrian memorandum, agreed completely with his imperial master. The Minister of War, von Falkenhayn, the Adjutant General, von Plessen, the Head of the Military Cabinet, von Lyncker, Captain Zenker of the naval staff, and Admiral von Capelle, representing von Tirpitz, were now successively called into the presence, and the question of "preparatory measures for war" was discussed with them on the evening of the 5th and the following morning, so as "to cover every case" before the Emperor left for Kiel to start his regular North Sea cruise. The question "whether the army was ready for any eventuality" was answered by von Falkenhayn with "a curt affirmative." On July 17 Major-General Count Waldersee, Quartermaster General in the general staff, who was then in the country, wrote to von Jagow in strict confidence: "I can move at a moment's notice. We in the general staff are *ready;* there is nothing more for us to do at this juncture." For the same reason Helmuth Count von Moltke, Chief of the General Staff, who had been informed by von Falkenhayn of the consultation of July 5 and by Lieutenant-Colonel Tappen of the Potsdam decision, found

it unnecessary to leave Karlsbad. How strongly the Emperor's decision had been influenced by his faith in the strength of Germany's
military forces is shown by what he said on July 6 to Capelle and
Lieutenant-General Bertrab of the general staff: France and Russia
were not ready for war; he did not believe in a general war, but
thought that now the army had been brought up to its present
strength, and with Germany's superiority in heavy artillery, he could
regard the outcome of a war with confidence (the campaign in the
west was expected to last 5–6 weeks). So, too, Waldersee said: "The
plans for mobilization had been duly completed on March 31, 1914;
the army was ready, as always."

"In order," as he said himself, "not to alarm world opinion," the
Emperor, after making all necessary dispositions, left for his North
Sea cruise. He did so in full awareness of the import of the assurances which he had given to Austria. Shortly after, when he was in
the company of Krupp von Bohlen and Halbach, with whom he was
on terms of intimacy, he assured him that:

> He would declare war at once, if Russia mobilized. This time people
> would see that he was not "falling out." The Emperor's repeated protes-
> tations that in this case no one would ever again be able to reproach him
> with indecision were almost comic to hear.

To understand the Emperor's insistence, we must remember the
criticisms of his attitude made by the military during the Morocco
crisis of 1911, and the *Alldeutsche* [Pan-German] threat that if he
again showed weakness, he would be deposed and replaced by the
Crown Prince.

While his imperial master was boarding the train for Kiel, Bethmann Hollweg, with Zimmermann in attendance, formally confirmed
to Hoyos and Szögyény the Emperor's decision of the previous day.
This gave constitutional cover to the "blank check." The Chancellor
left it to Austria to take the final decision but, like Wilhelm II, advised her to act at once, without informing Italy and Rumania; and
like the Emperor, he justified his course by appeal to the favorable
international situation. Szögyény had been prepared for this communication by the Emperor; Hoyos by Zimmermann, with whom he
had talked on the 5th. Hoyos had wanted military action against
Serbia *"sans crier gare,"* ["without warning"], and Zimmermann had

given him to understand that if Austria acted against Serbia at once, Russia and France would keep clear of the conflict. Any doubts or hesitations in Austria were removed when, on the 7th, Hoyos brought back Germany's unconditional promise to stand by Austria even if "measures against Serbia [which, Hoyos reported, Germany advised] should bring about the big war." The conditions for Conrad's plan were fulfilled.

A shift in the Hungarian Prime Minister's Austro-Hungarian policy came at a meeting of the Ministerial Council on July 7. All the participants except Tisza, who was still opposed to it, agreed on the necessity of war against Serbia, either by a direct attack without previous warning or by the presentation of an ultimatum with unacceptable demands which would equally lead to war. How strongly the decisions of the Council were influenced by the attitude of the Emperor and the German military is apparent from the answer given to Tisza by the Austrian Prime Minister, Count Stürgkh, who feared that "a policy of hesitation and weakness" would lose Austria Germany's support thereafter. When reporting to Franz Joseph two days later, Berchtold advised the ultimatum procedure, which would avoid "the odium of attacking Serbia without warning, put her In the wrong," and thus make it much easier for Rumania and Britain to preserve "at least [sic] neutrality." That he counted on the possibility of war with France and Russia is shown by the "long debate on the relative forces and the probable course of a European [sic] war" which we know from Hoyos' report and Conrad's notes to have taken place, although it was regarded as "not suitable for minuting."

Tisza, who on July 8 had still objected that an attack by Austria on Serbia would lead to "intervention by Russia and consequently world [sic] war," had, like Franz Joseph, been convinced by Germany's "unconditional attitude" that "the Monarchy had to reach an energetic conclusion." (When Tschirschky reported this, Wilhelm II added "certainly.") On the 14th Tschirschky was able to report that Tisza himself, the one opponent of war with "Serbia," had now agreed to a note "which would almost certainly be rejected [doubly underlined by Wilhelm II] and should result in war." So the first decision had been taken. That Germany faced the prospect of a general conflagration with open eyes emerges further from an instruction drafted by Radowitz, a Counsellor in the Foreign Ministry, as early as July 7 and sent by Jagow to Lichnowsky in London on the 14th.

Jagow warned the ambassador of the possibility of "general complications"; Germany wished to localize the Austro-Serbian conflict,
but not to prevent it. On the contrary, Lichnowsky was instructed to
mobilize the British press against Serbia, although he must be careful not to give the impression "that we were egging Austria on to
war." This epitomized German policy after the Hoyos mission. When
Tschirschky had reported on July 10 that Berchtold was now in favor
of "unacceptable demands," but that her "chief care" would now
be how to put these demands, the Emperor commented: "They had
time enough for that," and further made a suggestion which he
thought bound to succeed: "Evacuation of the Sanjak! Then the cat
is among the pigeons at once!"

German Pressure on Vienna

The mouthpiece in Vienna of Germany's pressure was her ambassador, Tschirschky, who from July 7 onwards was holding almost
daily discussions with the Ballhausplatz, on the proposed action
against Serbia. Tschirschky also attended the most important conferences between the Austrians, so that Vienna's decisions were
taken, literally, under his eyes.

After Austria had made up her mind to solve the Serbian question
by war, Tschirschky called on Berchtold on July 8 to give him another message from the Emperor, who wanted it "stated most emphatically that Berlin expected the Monarchy to act against Serbia,
and that Germany would not understand it if ... the present opportunity were allowed to go by ... without a blow struck."

As Berchtold reported, Tschirschky confirmed Stürgkh's fears that
hesitation by the Monarchy would destroy her value as an ally in
Germany's eyes. There was an implicit threat in his words when he
told Berchtold "that if we compromised or bargained with Serbia,
Germany would interpret this as a confession of weakness, which
could not be without effect on our position in the Triple Alliance
and on Germany's future policy." Tschirschky's influence can already
be traced in Berchtold's audience with the Emperor Franz Joseph
on July 9, for the Emperor consented to the minister's proposed
action on the ground that he feared "that a weak attitude would
discredit our position in Germany's eyes."

On July 11 Tschirschky, as he told Jagow in a strictly confidential private letter, "again took the occasion to discuss with Berchtold what action was to be taken against Serbia, chiefly in order to assure the minister once again, emphatically, that speedy action was called for."

The report by Berchtold on his interview with Tschirschky is supplemented and confirmed by a letter of July 12 from Szögyény. If it were possible *a priori* to think that Berchtold had invented his story of Tschirschky's pressure—the archives contain no telegram from Tschirschky confirming it—this suggestion would have to be dismissed in the light of the Emperor's marginal notes and Szögyény's dispatch. Szögyény fully confirmed Tschirschky's attitude. Germany, he wrote, Emperor and Chancellor alike, were pressing most vigorously for Austria to take immediate military action against Serbia. Szögyény believed that this "absolute" insistence on war against Serbia was based on the two considerations already mentioned: firstly, that Russia and France "were not yet ready" and, secondly, that Britain

will not at this juncture intervene in a war which breaks out over a Balkan state, even if this should lead to a conflict with Russia, possibly also France.... Not only have Anglo-German relations so improved that Germany feels that she need no longer fear a directly hostile attitude by Britain, but above all, Britain at this moment is anything but anxious for war, and has no wish whatever to pull the chestnuts out of the fire for Serbia, or in the last instance, for Russia.

Szögyény accordingly summarized his own views and those of Berlin in the following conclusion: "In general, then, it appears from all this that the political constellation is as favorable for us as it could possibly be." On the 13th Tschirschky was able to report: "Minister [Berchtold] is now himself convinced that immediate action called for." Wilhelm II received this communication (which he again underlined doubly) with obvious relief.

The other way in which Germany was exerting pressure on Austria was by insisting that the ultimatum to Serbia should be couched in terms so strong as to make acceptance impossible; here too the Emperor had given the cue on July 6, and here again his lieutenants followed his lead. As early as July 12 Germany was informed of the

contents of the Austrian note, and agreed that it should be delivered
about July 25, after Poincaré had left Petersburg. "What a pity!"
was the Emperor's comment on the lateness of the date.

Yet although Tisza had consented to military action—he expressly
emphasized that it was Germany's attitude that had decided him—
Vienna was still uncertain how sharp to make her demands on
Serbia. The Austrians had decided to make the ultimatum unacceptable, yet when Berchtold talked on July 17 to Prince Stolberg, Counsellor at the German embassy, he spoke as though it was not yet
quite certain whether Serbia would not after all accept the ultimatum. Stolberg reported to Bethmann Hollweg that he had had difficulty in concealing his displeasure at this hint that Austria might
weaken. His report continued:

> *If Austria really wants to clear up her relationship with Serbia once and*
> *for all, which Tisza himself in his recent speech called "indispensable,"*
> *then it would pass comprehension why such demands were not being*
> *made as would make the breach unavoidable. If the action simply peters*
> *out, once again, and ends with a so-called diplomatic success, the belief*
> *which is already widely held here that the Monarchy is no longer capable*
> *of vigorous action will be dangerously strengthened. The consequences,*
> *internal and external, which would result from this, inside Austria and*
> *abroad, are obvious.*

Jagow expressed the same train of thought the next day in a long
private letter to Lichnowsky. He was trying to answer the indirect
warning which Grey had had conveyed to Lichnowsky on July 9,
that Britain would never take the side of an aggressor, by explaining
why Germany thought sharp action by Austria against Serbia indispensable. First, he argued, war against Serbia was the Monarchy's
last chance of "political rehabilitation," for the Monarchy already
"hardly counted any more as a real great power." "This decline in
Austria's power position," he went on, "has also greatly weakened
our group of allies"; this was why he did not want, under any circumstances, to stop Austria from acting. He did not want to force a
preventive war, but should war come, he would not "jib at the
post," since Germany was militarily ready and Russia "fundamentally was not." The struggle between Teuton and Slav was bound
to come (a thought which often reappeared in Jagow's utterances
at critical junctures during the war); which being so, the present

was the best moment for Germany, for "in a few years Russia . . . will be ready. Then she will crush us on land by weight of numbers, and she will have her Baltic fleet and her strategic railways ready. Our group meanwhile is getting steadily weaker."

The argument that Germany was ready while Russia was not yet ready to strike, was especially emphasized by "German industrialists who specialize in armaments manufacture." Beyens, the Belgian ambassador in Berlin, reported that Krupp had assured him that "the Russian artillery was far from being either good or complete, while the German had never been better."

The Emperor, Bethmann Hollweg, Jagow and Zimmermann were all convinced of Germany's military superiority; so was the general staff. Count Lerchenfeld, the Bavarian minister in Berlin, reported at the end of July that Moltke had said that "a moment so favorable from the military point of view might never occur again." The reasons given by Lerchenfeld—which, he wrote, were by no means to be dismissed as "gossip between underlings"—were the familiar ones: superiority of German artillery and infantry rifle, insufficient training of the French army owing to the transition from the two to three years' term of service, the harvest in, and the training of the German first-line classes complete. For these reasons the politicians —Jagow, for example—could face the possibility of a European war with confidence: "If the conflict cannot be localized, and Russia attacks Austria-Hungary, this gives the *casus foederis.*"

If we study the documents and the political moves, Jagow's letter of July 18 to Lichnowsky puts Germany's attitude, and also the reasons for it, in a nutshell. It is impossible to speak seriously either of Germany's being "towed along in Austria's wake" or of her being "coerced." From the Emperor's first intervention in the Serbian question on July 4 to July 18, German policy followed an unbroken line, as nothing proves better than the constant assurances by Vienna that Berlin could rely on Austria-Hungary's willingness to fight—that there was "no question" of indecision or hesitation. But Germany's own aims were even plainer: if France proved too weak, militarily and financially, to support Russia, Bethmann Hollweg— so he hinted to Count Roedern, Secretary of State for Alsace-Lorraine and later of the German Treasury, on July 16—hoped at least to be able to divide France from Russia. Germany did not care so much what happened over Serbia; the central objective of her diplomacy in these weeks was to split the Entente, and this Bethmann Hollweg meant to enforce at any price, with or without war. In any case the Serbian crisis would bring about a regrouping of continental power relationships in a sense favorable to Germany and without intervention by Britain. The conflict must be localized, the great powers should "watch without acting," and Germany hoped to bring about a new grouping of forces in both the Balkans and the Mediterranean.

The German government, as Jagow informed Jules Cambon and Bronewski, the French ambassador and Russian chargé d'affaires in Berlin, on July 21, had no official information on Austria's aims or on its note. The Foreign Ministry, however, "entirely agreed that Austria must take advantage of the favorable moment, even at the risk of further complications," but both Jagow and Zimmermann, in obvious displeasure at Austria's weakness, doubted "whether Vienna would nerve herself to act." Zimmermann went so far as to transfer the description of "the sick man of Europe" from Turkey to Austria.

Berchtold confirmed the "nervousness" of the German statesmen. "Already," he wrote, "Berlin is beginning to get nervous." Reports were trickling through that Austria had hesitated too long before acting, and Zimmermann thought that "he had gathered the impression that Vienna, timid and undecided as it always was, was almost sorry"(!) that Germany was not pressing caution and moderation on her. Berchtold was pressing for action now. Conrad was urging "haste," and the Minister of War, Baron von Krobatin, said that "everything was ready for mobilization." The reason for haste was to prevent Serbia from "smelling a rat" and "herself volunteering compensation, perhaps under pressure from France and Russia." If that happened, then as Germany saw it, Austria-Hungary's reason for war against Serbia would vanish; but with it Germany would lose her minimum objective of a diplomatic victory, a major political success.

The Austrian Ultimatum to Serbia

After prolonged internal argument, the Austro-Hungarian Ministerial Council in Vienna decided on the final text of the ultimatum on July 19 and fixed the 23rd as the day for its delivery; both the Austrians and the Germans thought it prudent to wait until Poincaré and Viviani had left Petersburg, and thus prevent the French and Russians from agreeing immediately on their counter-measures. So active was the part played by Germany in the events of these days, so strong her influence over Austria-Hungary's policy, that Jagow actually had the time of the note's delivery on the 23rd put back an hour in order to make quite sure that the ship carrying the French statesmen had left Petersburg. The text of the note (the substance of which had been communicated to Germany on July 12) was conveyed by Tschirschky to the Foreign Ministry on the 22nd. If, as is often suggested, the Chancellor, Jagow or Zimmermann had found its wording too strong, they had time enough (from the evening of the 22nd to 6 p.m. on the 23rd) to protest against its presentation in that form. On the contrary: as late as July 18 Count Hoyos had reassured Prince Stolberg that the demands contained in the ultimatum "were *really* such as to make it *really* impossible" for the Serbian government to accept them with honor. As late as the 21st July Jagow had again assured Szögyény that Germany would stand behind Austria "unreservedly and with all her power." When he said that it was "vitally necessary" for Germany to know what Austria's plans for Serbia were, this was not out of any qualms about Austria's intentions, but because she wished, as Jagow put it to Tschirschky on the 17th, "to avoid giving any impression that we were wanting to impede Austria's actions, or to prescribe certain limitations or ends to her."

Now Germany waited for the presentation of the ultimatum.

The day before this was due, the purpose of the traveling about, of the "holiday spirit" of the military and political leaders of both Germany and Austria-Hungary, and of the efforts to keep the "Sarajevo spirit" alive, without, as Berchtold said, "making other powers begin thinking about mediation," became very plain. Vienna thought this the best way of keeping the Serbian action isolated. Germany, too, as Schoen, the Bavarian chargé d'affaires, told Munich (while passing on the three chief points of the ultimatum) wanted to make it look as though she was not a party to, or even informed about, what Vienna was doing. . . .

As early as July 21, Bethmann Hollweg and Jagow opened the official moves to localize the conflict with a circular dispatch. Even *before* the ultimatum had been presented, Berlin was instructing its embassies in Petersburg, Paris and London to support Austria's action, and was undisguisedly threatening the European powers with a major conflict if the Serbian question were not confined to Serbia and Austria. Austria's attitude, which had not yet been announced (it was only the *Norddeutsche Allgemeine Zeitung's* communiqué of the 19th which revealed to France the possibility of a major conflict), was "regarded as equitable and moderate," and Jagow now brought the whole discussion between Germany and Austria, including the underlying purposes, before the international forum in the following words:

> *If the Austro-Hungarian government is not going to abdicate forever as a great power, she has no choice but to enforce acceptance by the Serbian government of her demands by strong pressure and, if necessary, by resort to military measures. The choice of methods must be left to her.*

On the 23rd, however, Jagow realized that this dispatch was not easy to reconcile with the story that Germany had been "surprised" by Austria's action. A second dispatch, drafted by Stumm, was hurriedly sent after the first instructing the ambassadors not to make their *démarches* until the text of the ultimatum had been published: "otherwise the impression might be given that we had foreknowledge of it." The dispatch required the great powers to abstain from any intervention in the Austro-Serbian conflict, even threatening "incalculable consequences" if the warning were disregarded. This demand by Germany for a free hand for Austria surprised and displeased Grey, who did not believe that a war could be localized. In Germany, on the other hand, the conviction that Britain would stand aside from a European conflict was so firmly rooted that when Pourtalès, the German ambassador in Petersburg, reported Sazonov having told him that Britain would disapprove deeply of Austria's conduct, the Emperor wrote in the margin: "He's wrong"; and on Sazonov's warning that he must "reckon with Europe" in case of an attack on Serbia he commented: "No! Russia, yes!"

Yet, as innumerable documents show, Germany knew that Russia would never allow Austria-Hungary to act in the Balkans unopposed. She took the risk of war with open eyes. This is confirmed by the preparations taken by Germany when the ultimatum was presented to Serbia. Jagow, for example, asked for the exact itinerary of the imperial yacht, because:

> *Since we want to localize the conflict between Austria and Serbia, we must not have the world alarmed by His Majesty's returning prematurely; on the other hand, His Majesty must be within reach, in case unpredictable developments should force us to take important decisions, such as mobilization. His Majesty might perhaps spend the last days of his cruise in the Baltic.*

On July 20 the Directors General of the Hapag and the Norddeutscher Lloyd were, on the Emperor's suggestion and with the Chancellor's consent, given warning by Jagow of the impending ultimatum, so that they could take measures for the protection of their vessels in foreign waters. On the same day the Emperor ordered the concentration of the fleet.

Even before that 6 p.m. of July 23, 1914, when Baron Giesl, the Austrian minister in Belgrade, presented the ultimatum, the coming of war was assumed. On July 18 Count Hoyos had "comforted" Prince Stolberg with the assurance "that the demands [contained in the ultimatum] were *really* such as to make it *really* impossible for a state with any self-respect and dignity to accept them."[1]

Thus only unconditional acceptance by Serbia of the ultimatum could have averted war, and on July 22 Vienna asked Berlin how the declaration of war was to be effected, as Austria wanted her own answer to the rejection to consist of the rupture of diplomatic relations and the recall of her minister. She suggested that Germany might transmit the declaration of war. Jagow refused, saying that it would look too much "as though we had been egging Austria on to make war."

The "No" to British Mediation

The publication of the Austro-Hungarian ultimatum to Serbia evoked worldwide consternation except in Germany, where it was, in general, approved. The suspicion was often expressed that Germany was behind Austria's action, or at least privy to it. This suspicion

[1] Fischer's italics.—Ed.

was, as the German documents prove, completely justified, but Zimmermann denied it, as planned, in a telegram sent on the 24th to the German embassies in Paris, London and Petersburg. He asserted that Germany "had exercised no influence on the contents of the note" and had had "no more opportunity than any other power to take up any attitude towards it before its publication." The previous day Jagow had informed the Emperor that Grey had made his first attempt at mediation, suggesting to Lichnowsky that Britain should urge Russia to influence Serbia, and Germany to influence Austria-Hungary. The minutes with which the Emperor studded Lichnowsky's dispatch, which Jagow forwarded to him, show what he wanted quite clearly. His pent-up rage vented itself: Britain's "condescending orders" were to be rejected, and so was Grey's proposal that Vienna should retract any "impossible demands." "Am I to do that? Wouldn't think of it! What does he mean by 'impossible'? These fellows [the Serbs] have been intriguing and murdering, and they must be taken down a peg." He gave emphatic backing to the instructions from the Foreign Ministry which Jagow had sent to Lichnowsky "for guidance in your conversations." These show once more the consistency and purposefulness of German policy in July 1914. The ambassador was told that "we did not know what Austria was going to demand, but regarded the question as *an internal affair of Austria-Hungary, in which we had no standing to intervene.*"

As Sazonov had prophesied, the effect of the ultimatum on London was "absolutely annihilating." Lichnowsky reported that Britain believed that Germany, for all her protestations of innocence, was at least "morally an accomplice," and he went on to warn: "If we do not join in the mediation, all faith here in us and in our love of peace will be finally shattered." Germany, however, made no more than a pretense of supporting the vigorous action for mediation now initiated by Britain; indeed, in order to prevent the possibility of mediation, she actually sabotaged the proposals put forward by Britain between July 24 and the declaration of war. Her actions, and her motives, can be clearly followed, day by day, in the dispatches.

As early as July 24 Grey, alarmed by the provocative tone of the Austrian note and the shortness of the time limit, again warned Lichnowsky of the danger that "European war *à quatre*"—meaning, said Lichnowsky, Russia, Austria-Hungary, Germany and France—would break out if Austria crossed Serbia's frontiers. At the same

time he suggested mediation by the four powers not directly affected—Britain, France, Germany and Italy—in the event of "dangerous tension between Russia and Austria." Jagow, however, passed
on Grey's request for an extension of the time limit so late that it
reached Vienna only after the ultimatum had expired. Moreover, he
passed it on without comment, which in diplomatic parlance was
tantamount to asking that it should be rejected.

Grey initiated his second attempt at mediation on July 25 with his
old proposal that Berlin should intervene in Vienna to say that it
found Serbia's answer satisfactory. Again the proposal was passed
on without comment, although on the 25th Lichnowsky sent three
urgent messages advising Germany to give Austria "the hint." This is
not surprising: the Germans were furious with Berchtold for having
received the Russian chargé d'affaires on the 24th. "Quite superflu-
ous," commented the Emperor: "will give an impression of weakness.
Austria ... has ... taken the step, now it can't be sort of reconsidered
retrospectively."

Meanwhile, Petersburg had announced in an official communiqué
that it could not remain "uninterested" if Austria annexed Serbian
territory. The French and Russian ambassadors gave it as their personal opinions that Grey's proposal for four-power mediation in London was unacceptable, because the first step must be to mediate
between Austria-Hungary and Serbia and thus prevent a local war.
Germany accepted this latter proposal, not least in order to prevent
the "satisfactory line to England" from getting cut, especially at a
moment when Britain, France and Russia were not yet working as
one; Grey had stressed that he distinguished "sharply" between the
Austro-Serbian and the Austro-Russian conflicts and did not wish to
interfere in the Austro-Serbian affair. The British proposal thus meant
"localizing" the conflict, as Germany wished, and it was accordingly
answered affirmatively by Jagow late the same evening. On the 26th,
however, Bethmann Holweg, while not revoking the consent, threatened that Germany would mobilize if the reports of alleged call-up of
Russian reservists were confirmed. But the deeper reason for Germany's agreement, and for her policy—again announced by the Emperor—of "localizing the conflict" can be found in the documents of
the Foreign Ministry and of the Austrian embassy in Berlin. Germany's undoubted object was to thrust Russia far back. Tschirschky
had reported on the 24th that Austria wanted "no alteration in the

existing power relationships in the Balkans." The Emperor marked
this report "weak," and his notes on it reveal what were the objects
which Germany was following in the Serbian question: the alteration
of the Balkan power relationships, he wrote, "has got to come. Austria must become predominant in the Balkans . . . at Russia's expense." Szögyény confirmed that Germany's policy was to "localize
the conflict," but that she was aware that localization might prove
impossible, and was prepared to risk the consequences. "Here," he
reported, "it is generally taken for granted that if Serbia rejects our
demands, *we shall at once reply by declaring war* and opening military operations. We are advised . . . to confront the world with a *fait
accompli*." [2] On the 25th Giesl left Belgrade; Serbia's answer had
thus not been that demanded by Austria. On the same day Franz
Joseph signed the order mobilizing eight army corps. The 28th was
given as the first day of mobilization. Tisza, too, in an audience with
Franz Joseph, gave full support to the German pressure; hesitation
would "greatly impair belief in the Monarchy's energy and capacity
for action, in the eyes of both friend and foe."

On the 28th Lichnowsky transmitted yet another (the fourth) offer
of mediation, this time from King George V as well as Grey. He reported that "since publication of Austrian demands no one here believes any more in the possibility . . . of localizing conflict"; Britain
proposed a conference of ambassadors, "Britain and Germany working together, with France and Italy brought in . . . to secure Austria
full satisfaction . . . since Serbia would be more easily induced to
yield to pressure from the Powers and to submit to their united will,
than to Austria's threats." Grey and the Under-Secretaries, Nicolson
and Tyrell, saw in this procedure "the only possibility of avoiding
general war." "The absolute condition for success of the conference
and for maintenance of peace" was, however, "absence of any military dispositions."

If Serbia's territory was violated, Lichnowsky reported, "world war
could not be averted." Britain's disapproval of the line being followed
by Germany was equally unambiguous. "Localization of the conflict,
as hoped for by Berlin, was quite out of the question, and not to be
considered as practical politics." Lichnowsky urgently advised the
Foreign Ministry "to let our policy be determined singly and solely by

[2] Fischer's italics.—Ed.

the necessity of sparing the German people a struggle in which it has nothing to gain and everything to lose." In spite of these warnings, when Goschen, the British ambassador in Berlin, officially presented the proposal for a conference, Jagow rejected it. Even before this, Bethmann Hollweg had given a formal refusal in writing, on the ground that Germany "could not bring Austria's dealings with Serbia before a European tribunal." The Chancellor was not prepared to listen to Lichnowsky's representations, nor to follow Britain's change of course (meaning the dropping of the distinction between the Austro-Serbian and Austro-Russian conflicts). His replies to London continued to take, as sole basis, the British proposals for localizing the conflict. At the same time, a circular dispatch issued by him re-affirmed Germany's attitude that the conflict concerned only Austria-Hungary and Serbia.

The day before, Berchtold had told Austria's representatives to take the same line, and had added that if localization should prove impossible, Austria-Hungary was reckoning "with gratitude" that Germany "will support us if a struggle against another adversary is forced on us." Again on the 26th, Moltke had drafted a demand to Belgium to allow the passage of German troops in the event of "the imminent war against France and Russia," thereby proving plainly that Germany knew that war between Austria and Russia would imme-diately produce a continental war. Finally, on the 27th Grey sent an urgent appeal to Berlin to use its influence on Vienna to accept Serbia's answer as satisfactory, for only so could London, on its side, exercise a moderating influence on Petersburg. Lichnowsky reported that if war should after all break out, "it would no longer be possible to count on British sympathy or British support." Grey had said plainly that the key of the situation lay in Berlin; if Berlin was sincere in wanting peace, Austria could be prevented from following "a fool-hardy policy." Three hours later Lichnowsky repeated urgently that Grey was convinced that the maintenance of peace depended on Berlin. In London there was a steadily growing impression that "the whole Serbian question was developing into a trial of strength be-tween Triple Alliance and Triple Entente." If Austria-Hungary tried to beat Serbia into submission, Britain, said Lichnowsky, "would most certainly side with France and Russia" (the contents of this telegram were not shown either to Tschirschky or to the Emperor). Reports came in from Russia that Sazonov was being "more conciliatory," trying "to find a bridge . . . to satisfy . . . Austrian demands." Pourtalès reported, however, that the maintenance of the Balkan balance of power was a vital interest of Russia. Rome, too, reported the British proposals for mediation, and von Schoen telegraphed from Paris that France was ready to negotiate. The Quai d'Orsay would probably be ready to use its influence in Petersburg if Germany was prepared "to counsel moderation in Vienna, since Serbia had fulfilled nearly every point."

The Austro-Hungarian Declaration of War on Serbia

All these appeals and warnings failed to move Berlin to put any pressure on Vienna to avoid the local conflict. On the contrary, that same day—July 27—Berchtold, urged thereto by Germany, laid the declaration of war before Franz Joseph for his signature. He explained that, Serbia having answered as she had, the Entente might yet succeed in getting their proposals for mediation adopted "unless a clear situation was created by a declaration of war." Tschirschky reported to Berlin that the declaration of war would go off to Belgrade on July 28, or the 29th at the latest, "chiefly in order to eliminate any possibility of intervention."

This message reveals another feature of German policy in the July crisis. Not only did Germany consistently reject any attempt at mediation not calculated to "localize" the conflict, but while Grey and Sazonov were trying to gain time, Germany was pressing Austria to act quickly. As early as July 14 Vienna had intimated that it wanted to stop short of the irrevocable. In Berchtold's and Franz Joseph's eyes the ultimatum did not necessarily mean war, and Count Mensdorff, the Austrian ambassador in London, seemed not disinclined to accept Grey's offer of mediation. Germany, however, as she had stated *expressis verbis* on July 25, was pressing for a *fait accompli* to prevent other powers from intervening. When it received Tschirschky's report, the Wilhelmstrasse saw its goal achieved. The Chancellor accordingly adopted an attitude of reserve towards British pressure and showed no inclination to put quick and explicit pressure on Austria. It was only shortly before midnight that he passed on to Vienna the telegrams received that afternoon from London.

And before they were passed on Jagow had prepared the ground in another conversation with Szögyény. Again, as on July 18, he explained how Vienna was to interpret Germany's apparent change of course; again he confirmed the consistency and purposefulness of Germany's policy. Szögyény reported that, "in order to avoid any misunderstanding," Jagow had twice emphasized that:

> the German government assured Austria in the most binding fashion that it in no way identifies itself with the proposals [sc., the British proposals] which may very shortly be brought to Your Excellency's notice by the German government; it is, on the contrary, decidedly opposed to consideration of them, and is only passing them on out of deference to the British request.[3]

The Secretary of State himself was "absolutely against taking account of the British wish." At the same time, however, deference to Britain's wish was given as the pretext for the apparent acceptance. When explaining his point of view Jagow was more explicit still:

> The German government's point of view was that it was at the moment of the highest importance to prevent Britain from making common cause with Russia and France. We must therefore avoid any action which might cut the line, which so far had worked so well, between Germany and Britain.

Bethmann Hollweg confirmed Jagow's point of view when passing on to Tschirschky, late on the evening of the 27th, Lichnowsky's telegram on his interview with Grey:

> As we have already [sic] rejected one British proposal for a conference, it is not possible for us to refuse this suggestion also a limine. If we rejected every attempt at mediation the whole world would hold us responsible for the conflagration and represent us as the real warmongers. That would also make our position impossible here in Germany, where we have got to appear as though the war had been forced on us. Our position is the more difficult because Serbia seems to have given way very extensively. We cannot therefore reject the role of mediator; we have to pass on the British proposal to Vienna for consideration, especially since London and Paris are continuously using their influence on Petersburg.[4]

Bethmann Hollweg's and Jagow's point of view explains why the British telegram was passed on to Vienna so belatedly, and why the

---

[3] Fischer's emphasis.—Ed.
[4] Fischer's emphasis.—Ed.

last sentence was—characteristically—suppressed: it might conceivably have given the Austrian government another, eleventh-hour, chance of escaping out of the German stranglehold: "Also, the whole world here is convinced, and I hear the same from my colleagues, that the key to the situation lies in Berlin, and that if Berlin seriously wants peace, it will prevent Vienna from following a foolhardy policy."

But London was sent the completely untruthful message that: "We have immediately initiated mediation in Vienna in the sense desired by Sir Edward Grey."

The duplicity thus shown by the Chancellor in respect of Britain's grave warnings proves that in the night of July 27–28 he was no longer trying to avoid a continental war, but only to maneuver Germany into the most favorable position possible. If this aspect of Germany's policy had not emerged clearly enough from the judgment passed on the Anglo-German conversations by Bethmann Hollweg in his commentary when he forwarded Lichnowsky's telegram to Tschirschky, it is made still more plain from the fact that the Chancellor simultaneously forwarded to the Emperor the text of the British offer, with an exposé of Germany's attitude identical with that which had gone to Vienna. Although he wrote that he had "followed the Emperor's orders" in transmitting the British offer, he had in fact distorted the Emperor's intentions in his treatment of Grey's proposal: on returning from his North Sea cruise on the afternoon of July 27 and on reading Bethmann Hollweg's report that Germany had rejected the conference of ambassadors, Wilhelm had given orders that Grey's next proposal—for direct influence on Vienna—was to be accepted.

It was only on the 28th that the Emperor read Serbia's answer to the ultimatum, although the Serbian chargé d'affaires had handed it to the Foreign Ministry at noon on the 27th. The Emperor's comment confirmed Germany's policy once again: "*But* that eliminates any reason for war." Wilhelm's "halt in Belgrade" was issued independently of Grey's similar proposal. Since, however, he, unlike the Chancellor, was unaware that Austria's declaration of war on Serbia was imminent, he passed this proposal on to Jagow without much urgency. His opinion was: "The few reservations which Serbia has made with respect to certain points can in my opinion surely be cleared up by negotiation." This was the moment dreaded by the Foreign Ministry and by the military, the danger-hour which might see the monarch's weak nerve give way at the last moment, as it had in 1906 and 1911, before the certainty of war. Accordingly, he was now deliberately deceived. There is no other explanation for the fact that the Chancellor passed on this new suggestion too, belatedly, without urgency, and in distorted form. The only condition laid down by the Emperor in his "halt in Belgrade" was that Austria "had to have a guarantee that the promises were carried out." He thought this could be found in a *"temporary* occupation of parts of Serbia." In contradiction to this, Bethmann Hollweg emphasized to Tschir-schky that the occupation must be the means of compelling *"complete fulfillment* by the Serbian government of the Austrian demands." But the real falsification of the Emperor's proposals lay in Bethmann Hollweg's express insistence to Tschirschky:

> *You must most carefully avoid giving any impression that we want* to hold Austria back. *We are concerned only to find a* modus *to enable the realization of Austria-Hungary's aim* without at the same time unleashing a world war, *and* should this after all prove unavoidable, to improve as far as possible the conditions under which it is to be waged.[5]

"The War Guilt Is Russia's"

This addendum of July 28 reveals on the one hand the motives behind Germany's actions and on the other the Chancellor's conscious risk of a world war. For he himself explained what he meant by "favorable conditions": Firstly, Russia must be made to appear to blame for the outbreak of war, and secondly, Britain must be kept neutral. Bethmann Hollweg believed himself to have found the key to this problem in the "policy of localization." As early as July 26 he had expounded Germany's governing ideas very clearly both to the Emperor and to Pourtalès, Lichnowsky and Schoen, in the words: "Since Count Berchtold has assured Russia that Austria is not aiming at any territorial extensions in Serbia ... the maintenance of European peace depends exclusively on Russia." Germany's attitude must be "calm," for only if attacked could Germany count on British neutrality and carry public opinion at home with her, the chief need being to get the Social Democrats' support for war. From this point on the idea of making "Russia alone responsible for any extension of

[5] Fischer's emphasis.—Ed.

the conflict and disturbance of the European peace" appears with increasing frequence in the German documents. Jagow tried to influence the attitude of Italy, Rumania and Bulgaria in the event of a conflagration by asserting that both Germany and Britain were continually at pains to "keep the conflict localized" and that only Russia could begin the war.

The Chancellor took up this line of argument again in a memorandum sent by him on July 28, *qua* Prussian Prime Minister, to the Prussian legations at the German Courts. Again he defended Austria's conduct and underlined his policy of localizing the conflict. Just as Jagow, for example, writing to Bucharest on July 26, had alluded to the "obvious consequences" should Russia move against Austria, so Bethmann Hollweg ended his memorandum with the following passage:

> *Meanwhile should, contrary to our hopes, an intervention by Russia spread the conflagration, then we should be bound under our alliance to support our neighbor with the whole might of the Reich. Only under compulsion would we resort to the sword, but if we did so, it would be in calm assurance that we were guiltless of the sufferings which war might bring to the peoples of Europe.... Russia alone must bear the responsibility if a European war breaks out.*

Finally, the Chancellor drafted a telegram from the Emperor to the Tsar which reveals more clearly still his intention of saddling Russia with the odium of a "European conflagration." "If," he told the Emperor, "war should come after all, such a telegram would make Russia's guilt glaringly plain."

At 11 a.m. on July 28 Austria presented her declaration of war on Serbia. It was not until the afternoon that Tschirschky appeared with the Emperor's "halt in Belgrade." Berchtold rejected any intervention as too late. At the same time, however, tension had arisen between Vienna and Berlin. On July 27 Jagow had realized that Austria could not begin hostilities "in practice" until August 12. The German government found this delay regrettable, and in his telegram to Tschirschky of July 28, quoted above, Bethmann Hollweg explained the motives of German policy, which was not so much concerned to prevent a European war, as to avoid Austria getting herself saddled, out

of weakness and (as Lerchenfeld reported to Munich) political stupidity, with the odium of having herself provoked the war.

> *The Imperial government is thus put into the extraordinarily difficult posi-*
> *tion of being exposed during the intervening period to the other Powers'*
> *proposals for mediation and conferences, and if it continues to maintain*
> *its previous reserve towards such proposals, the odium of having pro-*
> *voked a world war will in the end recoil on it, even in the eyes of the*
> *German people. But a successful war on three fronts (viz., in Serbia,*
> *Russia and France) cannot be initiated and carried on on such a basis. It*
> *is imperative that the responsibility for any extension of the conflict to*
> *Powers not directly concerned should under all circumstances fall on*
> *Russia alone.*

The Chancellor held unwaveringly to his line: "localization" of the
conflict; should this prove impossible, then Russia must be branded
as the aggressor, thus to assure Britain's neutrality. The first object
was achieved: from the outbreak of the war to the present day, the
chief responsibility for it has been ascribed to Russia. The hope of
British neutrality was to prove a great illusion.

In spite of all Lichnowsky's warnings, the German government
continued to count confidently on British neutrality in a European
conflict. It also hoped that neither Italy nor Rumania would be able
to intervene actively against Germany. With Austria-Hungary's declaration of war, however, the diplomatic maneuverings reached the
critical stage when the event would show whether the confident attitude of Germany's diplomacy and the threat of her "gleaming sword"
would again tip the balance and secure localization of the conflict, as
in 1908–1909. The question whether localization was possible was
raised on the afternoon of July 28, when Conrad asked whether mobilization was to be carried through against Serbia alone, or also
against Russia; for he needed to know which the fronts were to be
by the fifth day of mobilization, or all the troop trains would be sent
towards Serbia. The "automatic operation of the war machine" now
began to show its effects in Germany, as well as Austria-Hungary.
Simultaneously with a call from Szögyény, bringing Conrad's request
for pressure on Russia (Berchtold already thought it essential for
both Austria and Germany to answer Russia's partial mobilization by
general mobilization), the Chancellor received a memorandum from

the general staff in which Moltke gave a clear and unambiguous analysis of the mechanics of mobilization and alliances and explained that they must inevitably lead to world war. Moltke emphasized particularly the causal nexus linking Austria's intervention against Serbia via Russian partial mobilization to Austrian, Russian and German general mobilizations, which would then inevitably draw in France, the first objective of German military strategy. The general staff's appreciation of the military position caused the Foreign Ministry to revise its view of the importance of Russia's partial mobilization (which the day before Jagow had not regarded as a cause for German mobilization). Up to this point Bethmann Hollweg had rejected as premature Austria's request for far-reaching military counter-measures, but under this pressure from Moltke and Conrad he addressed Petersburg in almost ultimatum terms, although the day before, Pourtalès had reported Sazonov as entirely ready to come an astonishingly long way to meet Austria's standpoint, which would have made possible some relaxation of the diplomatic tension. It was technically necessary for the military to get a clear picture of Russia's attitude, but Bethmann Hollweg's sharp tone was also clearly in line with the whole of German diplomacy during the July crisis. So long as England remained out—and it was hoped that a declaration of war by Russia would ensure this—the Chancellor was not in the least afraid of putting the Triple Alliance to the test of a European war.

As pendant to his strong attitude towards Russia, Bethmann Hollweg made every effort to appear in British eyes as the ardent searcher after peace. In two further interviews with Falkenhayn and Moltke, in the morning and the late evening of July 29, on each occasion before meeting the British ambassador, he succeeded in getting the proclamation of a state of emergency, for which the Prussian Minister of War was pressing, postponed, arguing that Germany must wait until Russia began general mobilization; for unless the blame for "the whole shlemozzle" could be pushed on to Russia, it was vain to hope for Britain's neutrality. If, however, Russia were saddled with the war guilt, Britain could not take her side. The generals, nevertheless, although still bound by the imperial "halt!" yet decided to send to the German minister in Brussels the demand (drafted on July 26) to allow the passage of German armies through Belgium.

In his morning conversation with Goschen on this day of July 29

Bethmann Hollweg again emphasized Germany's will for peace, and informed the ambassador in the strictest confidence of the Emperor's note to Vienna (Halt in Belgrade), again trying to give the impression that he was putting the brake on hard in Vienna, which, as we have seen, was in reality far from being the case. In the afternoon the Emperor consulted successively the Chancellor, Bethmann Hollweg, the Minister of War, von Falkenhayn, the Chief of the General Staff, von Moltke, the Head of the Military Cabinet, von Lyncker (4:40 p.m.), Grand Admiral Prince Henry (6:10 p.m.), the Secretary of State for the Navy, von Tirpitz, the Chief of the Naval Staff, von Pohl, and the Head of the Naval Cabinet, von Müller (7:15 p.m.). The conversations seemed to confirm Germany's hopes of British neutrality, for Prince Henry was able to report that George V ("Georgy") would remain neutral. The word of a king which the Emperor accepted, although von Tirpitz had doubts, brought the conversation round to France, Belgium and Holland. The Emperor emphasized that Germany wanted no territorial annexations from France, although his reasons reflected unspoken first war aims: Germany only wanted guarantees which should enable her to "prevent" further wars. Wilhelm built so largely on King George's reported word that (with Tirpitz's strong support) he rejected the proposal made by Bethmann Hollweg (who hoped to make the offer a sort of reward to Britain for her neutrality) for a naval agreement with Britain.

In his evening conversation with von Falkenhayn and von Moltke the Chancellor again insisted that Germany must wait until Russia ordered general mobilization or attacked Austria. For partial mobilization did not create a *casus foederis,* it did not necessarily involve war. Germany must wait for total mobilization, because only thereafter would both German and British public opinion support Germany's attitude in "the imminent war with Russia and France" (as the ultimatum to Belgium had already put it).

Germany concentrated her hopes ever more on getting Britain's promise of neutrality made contractual—as she had already tried to do on the occasion of the Haldane Mission. In the famous conversation between Bethmann Hollweg and Goschen late in the night of July 29–30 the Chancellor tried to pin Britain down by holding out prospects of a general agreement on neutrality. He assured Goschen: "We can assure the British Cabinet—*provided we are certain of their neutrality*—that even in case of a victorious war we shall not seek any territorial advantage in Europe at the expense of France"—a promise which, however, when Goschen raised the point, he refused to extend to France's colonies. Further, he declared himself ready to respect the neutrality and integrity of Holland, provided Germany's enemies would do the same. In speaking of Belgium, however, he betrayed Germany's intention of violating her neutrality by giving only the obscure assurance (which also agreed *verbatim* with the ultimatum) that Belgium's integrity (he did not mention her sovereignty) should not be impaired after the war "provided Belgium does not take sides against us"—provided, that is, Belgium did not resist Germany's illegal violation of her territory.

The British immediately grasped the decisive importance of this conversation. Now, Grey for the first time recognized Germany's intention of drawing the maximum political advantage from the Serbian conflict, even at the risk of European war. That on top of this Germany proposed to march through Belgium, Bethmann Hollweg had already admitted. Grey called the German offer "infamous." Similarly, Eyre Crowe, his right-hand man in the Foreign Ministry, concluded that Germany had practically made up her mind "to go to war." What had held her back hitherto had only been the fear that Britain would come to the help of France and Belgium. At the same time, however, the interview had revealed Germany's intentions; wrapped up as they had been, they could be recognized simply as the first stages of those German war aims which revealed themselves nakedly soon after the outbreak of the war: French colonies, in continuation of the policy of the second Morocco crisis of 1911; in respect of France herself Germany was binding herself only if Britain should remain neutral in a continental war (when she would make this sacrifice). In that case she would renounce annexations at the expense of France; but the implied converse of this observance was that if Britain entered the war, Germany, if victorious, would claim a free hand to annex French territory. The same reservation had been made also in respect of Belgium. Since Belgium resisted, Germany afterwards claimed a free hand there also; this reservation was already implicit in Bethmann Hollweg's words.

The position had been clarified. Germany had revealed her aims to Britain in the hope that the attempts made by both sides to reach a political settlement would now bear fruit. The conversation also marked the high watermark of Germany's "policy of localization"; the dispatch in which Goschen reported the conversation, the verbal accuracy of which he got the Chancellor to check immediately afterwards, showed no sign of compromise either in tone or in substance. It was only after the British ambassador, who, as he said himself, had hardly been able to repress his astonishment but had raised no objections, had left the room, that Bethmann Hollweg received Lichnowsky's telegram, which had arrived earlier but had only now been deciphered. Its contents for the first time shook the whole structure of Bethmann Hollweg's diplomacy, the corner-stone of which had been the hope of British neutrality.

The Collapse of Bethmann Hollweg's Policy

Lichnowsky reported that Grey had again repeated with extreme earnestness his proposal for four-power mediation, and had emphasized that Britain, as a neutral power, was prepared, if Germany helped her, to mediate between Austria-Hungary on the one side and Serbia and Russia on the other, but that the moment France was drawn into the war, Britain would *not* be able to stand aside. This upset the calculation on the basis of which Germany had urged Austria to take military action against Serbia and believed herself capable of regarding the prospect of European war "with equanimity" in the confident hope that Britain would after all remain neutral if the responsibility for the war were laid on Russia. Now the situation suddenly became threatening. Only three days before Jagow had confidently told Jules Cambon, who thought that Britain would intervene immediately: "You have your information, we have ours; we are certain of British neutrality." The Germans, Bethmann Hollweg most of all, were surprised, even shattered, by Lichnowsky's report, and they grew unsure of themselves. The foundation of their policy during the crisis had collapsed. Britain would not remain neutral if France were "drawn into" the war. The telegram sent to Tschirschky at 3 a.m. on the 30th to inform him of Lichnowsky's message described the new situation:

> *If, therefore, Austria should reject all mediation, we are faced with a conflagration in which Britain would be against us, Italy and Rumania in all probability not with us. We should be two Great Powers against four. With Britain an enemy, the weight of the operations would fall on Germany. . . . Under these circumstances we must urgently and emphatically suggest to*

the Vienna cabinet acceptance of mediation under the present honorable conditions. The responsibility falling on us and Austria for the consequences which would ensue in case of refusal would be uncommonly heavy.

Only five minutes later Bethmann Hollweg sent a telegram to Vienna in which he summoned his ally even more energetically to stop "refusing any exchange of views with Russia." "We are prepared," he went on, "to fulfill our duty as allies, but must refuse to allow Vienna to draw us into a world conflagration frivolously and without regard to our advice."

These two documents, composed simultaneously and dispatched to Vienna in the small hours, are used, together with Bethmann Hollweg's address to the Prussian Ministry of State on the afternoon of the same July 30, to prove the peaceable nature of Germany's policy and to show the "absolutely desperate efforts" made by Bethmann Hollweg to make Vienna retreat. But the significant thing about them is not so much Bethmann Hollweg's urgent attempt to get Vienna to accept the British proposals as the fact that they find no parallel among the documents of the night of July 29–30 or of July 30 itself. The first dispatches to go out after the arrival of the news from London, they are the products of the shock born of the unexpected information about Britain's attitude.

As late as 11:05 p.m. on the 29th Bethmann Hollweg, completely consistently with his previous policy of "localization," had summoned Russia in almost ultimatum terms "not to provoke any warlike conflict with Austria." At 12:30 a.m. he informed Vienna of Russia's partial mobilization and added: "To avert a general catastrophe, or" —and this shows clearly the tactics consistently followed by German civilian policy, uninfluenced by the Emperor or the general staff—"*in any case* to put Russia in the wrong, we must urgently wish Vienna to begin and continue conversations [with Russia] in accordance with telegram 174." [6] The deductions drawn by the Chancellor from the "Russian mobilization" are astonishing, for telegram 174 was that sent by Jagow to Tschirschky on the 28th, which gave Vienna its first information of the British proposals for mediation, but with the characteristic addition: "You must avoid most carefully giving any impression that we want to hold Austria back." Up to the morning of

[6] Fischer's italics.—Ed.

July 30 Berlin had followed its policy of absolutely pressing action on Austria. It was only after 12:30 a.m. that Bethmann Hollweg saw Lichnowsky's report from London; this he sent on to Vienna at 2:55 a.m. with the first urgent warning. This telegram, however, also explains what the German "advice" for the prevention of the "world conflagration" really came to. Austria-Hungary was thus not being at all "tough" (*pace* Gerhard Ritter) or obstinate, or set on war, and Germany was not being dragged in her wake. Furthermore, Austria-Hungary had involved herself so deeply in the crisis that neither Berchtold nor Tisza thought it possible for her, as a great power, to give way now to German pressure which, moreover, was not applied with the whole weight available to Germany. Moreover, Vienna had, as the discussions went on, grown ever more convinced that the way to strengthen the structure of the Monarchy was by way of a war covered by Germany.

But this is not the only circumstance revealing the exceptional character of the documents; there are also the warnings given in the course of July 30. For the very next documents show plainly that what chiefly concerned Bethmann Hollweg was not so much to save the peace as such as to shift the responsibility and guilt for the war onto Russia. But the essential point was that although the premises of Bethmann Hollweg's policy, his conditions for undertaking war, as laid down by him on July 5 and 6, had collapsed, he could not steel himself to change his policy, to talk unambiguously to Vienna and to force it to obey him. A declaration to this effect, combined with a threat to leave Austria alone if she disregarded it, could have saved the Reich from the catastrophe of a war waged under conditions which had become so unfavorable. But nothing was done. On the contrary, the old policy was resumed in the course of the 30th.

This emerges clearly from the record of the meeting of the Prussian Ministry of State on July 30, to which Bethmann Hollweg reported on the situation. His main preoccupation was again "to *represent* Russia as the guilty party," and this, he thought, would be most easily achieved if Vienna accepted Germany's suggestion, namely, to assure Petersburg that she meant only to occupy parts of Serbia temporarily, as guarantee for the satisfaction of her demands. But it also emerges clearly why Bethmann Hollweg was still continuing to insist on Russia's "war guilt." Previously his chief motive had been to secure Britain's neutrality—a hope which, he now remarked bitterly, had practically disappeared; the second factor in his "mission" as Chancellor (second to the *rapprochement* with Britain) now came increasingly into the foreground. If the declaration of war came from Russia, he said, there was "nothing to fear" from the Social Democrats. "There will be no question of a general or partial strike, or of sabotage." The British intervention had shifted the emphasis in his motives, no more. This appears plainly in the dispatch sent that evening to Vienna and in its cancellation, which also affected indirectly the German move taken in the course of the night.

> *If [the Chancellor wired to Tschirschky on the evening of July 30] Vienna ...refuses...to give way at all, it will hardly be possible to place the blame on Russia for the outbreak of the European conflagration [not to prevent the war, but to place the blame on Russia]. H.M. has, on the request of the Tsar, undertaken to intervene in Vienna, because he could not refuse without awakening an irrefutable suspicion that we wanted war.*

Alluding to Britain's attempts to mediate in Paris and Petersburg, he went on:

> *If these efforts of Britain's meet with success, while Vienna refuses everything, Vienna will prove that it is set on having a war, into which we are dragged, while Russia remains free of guilt. This puts us in a quite impossible position in the eyes of our own people. We can therefore only urgently recommend Vienna to accept Grey's proposal, which safeguards its position in every way.*

The telegram stresses once again the cardinal importance of British neutrality, of Russian war guilt and of national solidarity as the factors governing German policy. Yet Germany's peaceful protestations to Britain were purely tactical, as is made plain by the fate of a telegram from King George to Prince Henry suggesting cooperation between Germany and Britain to save the peace. This telegram arrived just before midnight (11:08 p.m.) on July 30. Vague as was the glimmer of hope which it offered that Britain might remain neutral, it was enough for Bethmann Hollweg to cancel his demand that Vienna should "accept Grey's proposal" only twelve minutes later (11:20 p.m.). At the same time the Chancellor completely lifted such pressure—and it had been weak enough—as he had been putting on Vienna. No proof could be plainer of the tactical nature of Germany's "peace moves." Comparison with the instructions sent to

Tschirschky makes this more glaring still. Telegram No. 200 called on Vienna to accept mediation, since otherwise Russia "would bear no blame." Telegram No. 201, sent by Jagow in the same hour, rejected Austria's proposal for a joint *démarche* in Paris and Petersburg on the ground that Germany "could not take the same step again." Telegram No. 202 cancelled telegram No. 200. Telegram No. 203 explained telegram No. 202, and telegram No. 204 on July 31 demanded Austria's "immediate participation in the war against Russia."

Besides explaining the cancellation telegram by King George's message, Bethmann Hollweg had also drafted, although not yet sent, a military explanation which ran: "I have cancelled execution of instructions in No. 200, because the General Staff has just informed me that military measures by our neighbors, especially in the east, compel speedy decision if we are not to be taken by surprise." This alluded to the military considerations which became more and more prominent on July 30 and acquired great cogency when the news of Russia's partial mobilization arrived.

The Beginning of World War

That the two demands sent to Vienna—for tactical reasons, and by no means in any "desperate endeavor to save the peace"—to accept the British proposals constitute an isolated episode, a hesitation in view of Britain's attitude, appears more plainly than ever if we turn to the steps initiated by Moltke when the news of Russia's partial mobilization against Austria-Hungary arrived. As late as July 29, Moltke and Falkenhayn postponed the proclamation of a "state of imminent war," in obedience to the Emperor's orders and out of deference to Bethmann Hollweg's hopes of British neutrality, but on the morning of July 30 all such considerations were swept aside when the Foreign Ministry (presumably Zimmermann) passed on to the general staff the Emperor's marginal notes on Pourtalès' report that Russia had ordered partial mobilization. Wilhelm's comment on Sazonov's announcement that Russia was "mobilizing against Austria" was: "Then I must mobilize too," and he went on: "Then he [sc., Tsar Nicholas II] is taking on himself the guilt" (for a European war). . . . "I regard my attempted mediation as having failed." In such theatrical wise did Wilhelm II lay down what on another occasion he called his "office of mediator," an office which he had in reality never assumed. The Chancellor thereupon informed the Emperor "that any explanation given by Vienna to Petersburg on the purpose and extent of Austria's measures against Serbia [which he urged Berchtold to give] could only make Russia's guilt heavier and prove it more clearly to the whole world." Thus did Bethmann Hollweg again interpret to the Emperor on July 30 the governing principles of his policy.

But the noonday hours of July 30 are important in other respects also. During these hours the Emperor received further information both on the Russian partial mobilization and on Britain's attitude, the latter supported by a report from the naval attaché in London that "the British fleet will launch an *instant and immediate attack on us at sea* if it comes to war between us and France." This report caused the Emperor extraordinary consternation and disillusionment. He and Prince Henry had just been concocting an answer to King George, based on his first message that "we shall try all we can to keep out of this and to remain neutral." He had hoped very long that Britain would remain neutral, but when the dispatches reached him—very, very belatedly—the situation changed. Their effect on Bethmann Hollweg was to cause temporary hesitations and retreats; on the Emperor it was the opposite. His naked hatred of "perfidious Albion," of "that filthy cur, Grey," of "that filthy nation of grocers" vented itself with elemental violence. "England drops the mask the moment she thinks we are safely in the corral and done for, so to speak." He now discovered who was the real war criminal, for Russia would never have been able to begin the war without England's support. "England alone is responsible for war and peace, not we any more!" The Emperor's marginal notes grow more and more sweeping. Germany is encircled; the war of annihilation has been concerted; Germany is to go under; all this is purposeful "anti-German world policy"; "and there have been people," he writes in sarcastic allusion to the Chancellor, "who have believed it possible to win over or appease England by one petty concession or another! ! ! And we have put our heads into the noose and have even introduced the slow march in our naval program in the pathetic hope that this would placate England! ! !" Wilhelm II felt himself betrayed and double-crossed. "Edward VII dead is stronger than I am alive." At the same time, however—and this is the further and historic importance of Grey's warning and of Pourtalès' reports—his long-harbored idea turned into the conscious purpose of destroying the British Empire by unleashing revolution in the Mohammedan world. . . .

First, however, the Emperor's attitude had enabled the military to begin action in Prussia and Germany. Since Russia's partial mobilization did not yet constitute, in German eyes, sufficient ground for Germany to initiate general mobilization, Moltke pressed Austria-Hungary to adopt instant general mobilization without, however, declaring war on Russia, since the *casus foederis* for Germany would only arise if Russia declared war—and if Russia declared war, Moltke still believed that Britain would keep out. When, then, at 11:50 a telegram from Pourtalès revealed the *extent* of Russian partial mobilization, the military were alerted. Nevertheless, when Bethmann Hollweg met Falkenhayn and Tirpitz at noon on the 30th, he succeeded once again in securing postponement of the proclamation of "imminent threat of war" on grounds of internal policy. Moltke, however, who had attended the meeting uninvited, now took independent action. He sent an urgent warning to Conrad to mobilize immediately against Russia (letting the dispositions against Serbia take second place) and to announce as his reason the Russian proclamation of partial mobilization ("thus," according to Ritter, "making Russia appear the aggressor"). Only "so would the *casus foederis* for Germany arise." Britain's latest step to preserve the peace must be rejected. "To last out a European war" was "the last means of preserving Austria-Hungary." "Germany will come in under all circumstances." In the evening Moltke repeated his demands and sent the assurance that "Germany would mobilize." Szögyény reported that "till recently, all authoritative circles here had regarded the possibility of a European conflict with the most complete calm." Since July 30 signs of nervousness had become apparent, but the reason was not nervousness over the outbreak of a European war, but "anxiety lest Italy might fail to fulfill her obligations towards her partners in the Triple Alliance in the event of a general conflict." It was only because Berlin and Vienna "absolutely needed Italy if they were to be safe in entering a general conflict" that Germany was repeatedly pressing Vienna—as Moltke did twice on the 30th—to go to the limit in meeting Italy over the question of compensation.

At 9 p.m. on the 30th Bethmann Hollweg and Jagow yielded to

Moltke's and Falkenhayn's insistence that the "state of imminent war" must be proclaimed by noon on the next day at the latest. At midnight, only three hours after the evening meeting, Moltke had his adjutant, von Haeften, draft the Emperor's proclamation to his people, his army and his navy. At 9 a.m. on July 31 it was agreed that the order for the measures of mobilization consequent on this proclamation should be issued if Russia's general mobilization was confirmed.

The report of Russia's general mobilization was confirmed at noon on July 31. In the afternoon the Emperor, speaking from a balcony of the Palace, proclaimed a "state of imminent threat of war," declaring that "they are pressing the sword into our hand," Bethmann Hollweg's courage in waiting for Russia to order general mobilization had thus reaped its reward: the German people was ready for war in the conviction that it had been gratuitously assailed. Sazonov had put this trump into his hand. By making Russia appear the guilty party, Bethmann Hollweg had also been able to eliminate the possibility of opposition from the Social Democrats. On the 31st Lerchenfeld reported to Munich, sarcastically but with relief, that the Social Democrats had "in duty bound, demonstrated in favor of peace," but were now "keeping quite quiet." This was also the purpose of giving Russia twelve hours' notice in the ultimatum, and of the postponement until August 1 (made possible by the perfection of her dispositions) of Germany's general mobilization.

At the very last hour it again appeared possible that Bethmann Hollweg's policy might bear fruit and Britain remain neutral. On August 1, after the order for mobilization had been signed, an offer arrived from London to guarantee France's neutrality. This seemed to hold out the prospect of war on a single front. The Emperor accepted the offer and ordered Moltke "to hold up the advance westward." There followed the famous scene which exposed the utter helplessness of Germany's military rigidity. Moltke protested against the Emperor's order, saying that the only up-to-date plan of campaign (the famous Schlieffen Plan, revised by him in 1913) provided for attack only against France. Nevertheless the Emperor ordered that the advance, which had already begun—patrols had penetrated into Luxemburg—was to be halted. Moltke was beside himself at the possibility of France remaining neutral and said that if the advance into France did not take place, he could "undertake no responsibility for the war." "Now," he remarked bitterly, as we know from the recollections of the Head of the Naval Cabinet, "it only remains for Russia to back out, too." After sharp argument, the Chancellor and the Chief of the General Staff ended by agreeing that the advance would have to go on "for technical reasons." Britain's offer had come too late. Yet the illusion persisted and even gathered strength. A second telegram from Lichnowsky on the same day suggested a possibility that Britain might remain neutral even in a war between Germany and both Russia and France. "What a fabulous turn of events," reported Müller "the Emperor was delighted, and called for champagne," as was his habit later, during the war, to celebrate real or imagined victories. Bethmann Hollweg's policy seemed to have succeeded. Germany could engage Russia and France at her ease. But these hopes were to prove short-lived.

The subsequent disillusionment served to inflame still further Germany's hatred of Britain, which now became almost unbounded. On the other hand, it cleared the way for the westward advance as foreseen in the Schlieffen Plan. Italy having declared neutrality, the Germans began the World War in the face of the most unfavorable possible grouping of the powers. The declaration of war on Russia on August 1 and on France on August 3, punctilious as they were from the bureaucratic point of view and devastating as were their effects on opinion elsewhere in the world, nevertheless only marked the formal end of the complex process which had led up to them. In this respect, too, it is characteristic that Austria-Hungary's declarations of war on Russia and on the Western Powers followed only a week later, under German pressure, and that Germany's declaration of war had long since started on its journey when the Tsar telegraphed again to express confidence that peace could still be preserved in spite of the mobilizations. The violation of Belgium's neutrality enabled the British government to win over parliament and people for immediate entry into the war, a decision politically motivated by the often expressed determination not to allow Germany to overthrow France and leave Britain to face alone a continent dominated by Germany.

Who Was "Guilty"?

There is no question but that the conflict of military and political interests, of resentment and ideas, which found expression in the

July crisis, left no government of any of the European powers quite free of some measure of responsibility—greater or smaller—for the outbreak of the war in one respect or another. It is, however, not the purpose of this work to enter into the familiar controversy, on which whole libraries have been written, over the question of war guilt, to discuss exhaustively the responsibility of the individual statesmen and soldiers of all the European powers concerned, or to pass final judgment on them. We are concerned solely with the German leaders' objectives and with the policy actually followed by them in the July crisis, and that only insofar as their policy throws light on the postulates and origins of Germany's war aims.

It must be repeated: given the tenseness of the world situation in 1914—a condition for which Germany's world policy, which had already led to three dangerous crises (those of 1905, 1908 and 1911), was in no small measure responsible—any limited or local war in Europe directly involving one great power must inevitably carry with it the imminent danger of a general war. As Germany willed and coveted the Austro-Serbian war and, in her confidence in her military superiority, deliberately faced the risk of a conflict with Russia and France, her leaders must bear a substantial share of the historical responsibility for the outbreak of general war in 1914. This responsibility is not diminished by the fact that at the last moment Germany tried to arrest the march of destiny, for her efforts to influence Vienna were due exclusively to the threat of British intervention and, even so, they were half-hearted, belated and immediately revoked.

It is true that German politicians and publicists, and with them the entire German propaganda machine during the war and German historiography after the war—particularly after Versailles—have invariably maintained that the war was forced on Germany, or at least (adopting Lloyd George's dictum, made for political reasons, that "we all stumbled into the war") that Germany's share of the responsibility was no greater than that of the other participants. But confidential exchanges between Germany and Austria, and between the responsible figures in Germany itself, untinged by any propagandist intent, throw a revealing spotlight on the real responsibility.

A few weeks after the outbreak of war, during the crises on the Marne and in Galicia, the Austrians asked urgently for German help against the superior Russian armies facing them. It was refused. Count Tisza then advised Berchtold to tell the Germans: "That we took our decision to go to war on the strength of the express statements both of the German Emperor and of the German Imperial Chancellor that they regarded the moment as suitable and would be glad if we showed ourselves in earnest."

Just three years later, on August 14, 1917, at the climax of a heated debate whether the war should be continued in the interest of Germany's war aims, Austria-Hungary's Foreign Minister, Count Czernin, told his German interlocutors excitedly: "It was not Austria alone that began the war then." Characteristically, the official German minutes in the Imperial Chancellery left Czernin's next sentence incomplete and passed over the retorts of the German statesmen, Michaelis, Kühlmann and Helfferich, but the minutes of the Army High Command (the OHL) gave the sentence in full: "Germany demanded that the ultimatum to Serbia should be drawn up in those sharp terms."

In February 1918, again, Czernin asked Berchtold if he would object if he (Czernin) published a letter written by him to Tisza shortly before the outbreak of war, which showed "what strong efforts Germany was making at that time to hold us to a hard line, and how our alliance might have been in danger if we had given way."

There is other evidence to confirm that the Central Powers in no way "slid into war." Josef Baernreither, an Austrian politician who was entirely well disposed towards the Reich and was a leading champion of the Mitteleuropa idea during the war, made the following entry on the July crisis in his diary for December 1914:

The Germans were afraid that we would refuse to go with them if the war broke out over some question remote from us. At Algeciras we were still "seconds": later, not even that; in the Morocco crisis we did not stand by Germany firmly. But war was bound to come, as things had developed, through the faults of German and Austro-Hungarian diplomacy. So when the Sarajevo murder took place, Germany seized her opportunity and made an Austrian grievance her signal for action. That is the history of the war.

Finally, on October 8, 1919, Czernin telegraphed to Karl H. von Wiegand (the Berlin correspondent of the *Herald and Examiner*) the following reply to questions addressed to him by Wiegand:

Repeated conversations and interviews I had with Ambassador von Tschirschky could create no other impression than that his [the German] government expected warlike action on our part against Serbia. Especially a conversation I had with him during the early half of July convinced me that if we did not show this time that we were in earnest, then on the next occasion Berlin not only would not support us, but would in fact "orient" itself in some other direction.

What that would have meant for us, in view of the ethnographical composition of the Dual Monarchy and the territorial aspirations of our neighbor states, need not be explained.

Tschirschky was informed about the material points in the ultimatum to Serbia before the final editing of the note and the textual contents were given to him two days before the Belgrade démarche.

Baernreither was confirmed in his view of the nature of the July crisis by a conversation which he had in November 1915 with Otto Hoetzsch of Berlin, the historian of eastern Europe, leader-writer for the *Kreuzzeitung* and later German National deputy in the Reichstag. "Then" (sc., after July 5, 1914), runs the entry in Baernreither's diary, "the Emperor went off to Norway, knowing certainly that war would break out. Germany had arranged all this very cleverly, and had shown alertness and judgment in picking an occasion when she was certain of Austria's support in waging a war the inevitability of which had been becoming apparent for years past."

A week later Hoetzsch's Berlin colleague, the economist Jastrow, confirmed the correctness of Hoetzsch's view to Baernreither.

Arthur von Gwinner, Director of the Deutsche Bank, again confirmed most clearly the will to risk war which existed in Germany, especially in the Foreign Ministry, in a conversation which he had on the July crisis at the end of August 1914 with von Capelle, the Under-Secretary of State in the Reich Naval Office. He, too, stressed the factor of Austria's unreliability:

The only reason why Lichnowsky was not informed was because here [in the Wilhelmstrasse] they were determined to force a conflict. When Capelle asked who had been the man behind this pressure, Gwinner answered, "Herr von Stumm, in the Foreign Office, for example." When Capelle expressed some doubt, he went on: "Perhaps it was a whole group. They worked systematically to get Austria committed inextricably, as the first step, so as to be sure of her. The whole plan of campaign against Serbia was arranged in advance to make a conflict inevitable."

This grave statement was published as early as 1926 by no less a man than Grand Admiral von Tirpitz, in his *Deutsche Ohnmachts-*

politik (Germany's Policy of Weakness), but it has, so far as the author knows, passed unnoticed.

Admiral Müller, commenting in his diary on the Entente's answer of December 31, 1916, to the German peace offer—a document which ascribed to Germany a substantial share of the guilt for the World War—wrote that it "contained certain bitter truths on our doings at the outbreak of the war."

Finally Albert Ballin, Bethmann Hollweg's and Jagow's intimate political confidant (he was sent to London by Jagow at the beginning of the crisis of July 1914, in an attempt to secure Britain's neutrality, and was summoned to Berlin in the middle of 1915 to help draft Germany's note to the United States which was to decide on peace or war with America but was not received by Jagow after all), wrote at that date to the Secretary of State, out of his intimate knowledge of what had been done in July 1914:

> *I make every allowance for a man who is heavily incriminated, as Your Excellency is, and has to bear the frightful responsibility for having staged this war* [für die Inscenierung dieses Krieges] *which is costing Germany generations of splendid men and setting her back 100 years.*

The official documents afforded ample proofs that during the July crisis the Emperor, the German military leaders and the Foreign Ministry were pressing Austria-Hungary to strike against Serbia without delay, or alternatively agreed to the dispatch of an ultimatum to Serbia couched in such sharp terms as to make war between the two countries more than probable, and that in doing so they deliberately took the risk of a continental war against Russia and France. But the decisive point is that, as we now know—although for a long time it was not admitted—these groups were not alone. On July 5 and 6 the Imperial Chancellor, Bethmann Hollweg, the man in whom the constitution vested the sole responsibility, decided to take the risk and even over-trumped the Emperor when he threatened to weaken. That this was no "tragic doom," no "ineluctable destiny," but a deliberate decision of policy emerges beyond doubt from the diary of his private secretary, Kurt Riezler, who recorded in it his conversations with the Chancellor in the critical days (and, indeed, over many years). These diaries have not yet been published, but the extracts from them which have seen the light furnish irrefutable proof that during the July crisis Bethmann Holl-

weg was ready for war. More than this. Riezler's entry for the evening of July 8, after Bethmann Hollweg's return to Hohenfinow
(where Rathenau was also stopping) shows what advance calculations the leaders of Germany were making in respect of the situation
produced by the Sarajevo murder. According to his secretary, the
Chancellor said: "If war doesn't come, if the Tsar doesn't want it
or France panics and advises peace, we have still achieved this
much, that we have maneuvered the Entente into disintegration over
this move."

In other words, Bethmann Hollweg reckoned with a major general
war as the result of Austria's swift punitive action against Serbia. If,
however, Russia and France were again to draw back (as in 1909
and 1911)—which he at first regarded as the less probable eventuality—then at least Germany would have achieved a signal diplomatic victory: she would have split Russia from France and isolated
both without war. But war was what he expected, and how he
expected its course to run we learn from his predecessor in the
Chancellorship, Bülow, who had a long discussion with him at the
beginning of August. Bethmann Hollweg told Bülow that he was
reckoning with "a war lasting three, or at the most, four months . . .
a violent, but short storm." Then, he went on, revealing his innermost
wishes, it would "in spite of the war, indeed, through it," be possible
to establish a friendly relationship with England, and through England with France. He hoped to bring about "a grouping of Germany,
England and France against the Russian colossus which threatens
the civilization of Europe."

Bethmann Hollweg himself often hinted darkly during the war how
closely Germany had been involved in the beginning of the war. He
was less concerned with the "staging" of it than to register the spirit
of the German leaders who had made it possible for the war to be
begun even after the premises for it had collapsed. The following
bitter words are taken from his address to the Central Committee of
the Reichstag at the beginning of October 1916, during the sharp
debate on the initiation of unlimited submarine warfare; they outline
Germany's real "guilt," her constant overestimation of her own
powers, and her misjudgment of realities:

> *Since the outbreak of the war we have not always avoided the danger of*
> *underestimating the strength of our enemies. The extraordinary develop-*
> *ment of the last twenty years seduced wide circles into overestimating*

our own forces, mighty as they are, in comparing them with those of the rest of the world . . . in our rejoicing over our own progress [we have] not paid sufficient regard to conditions in other countries.

The July crisis must not be regarded in isolation. It appears in its true light only when seen as a link between Germany's "world policy," as followed since the mid-1890s, and her war aims policy after August 1914.

Gerhard Ritter
A NEW WAR-GUILT THESIS?

When Gerhard Ritter, Professor of Modern European History at Freiburg from 1924–1956, died on July 1, 1967, he had completed the manuscript of the fourth volume of his monumental work, Staatskunst und Kriegshandwerk: das Problem des Militarismus in Deutschland [Statecraft and the Arms Profession: The Problem of Militarism in Germany]. *Although he belonged to the older generation of German historians who had lived through the war-guilt controversy of the twenties and thirties, he admitted that German war-guilt literature needed revision, but could not accept Fischer's thesis. The selection below was published in 1962 in criticism of the first edition of Fischer's book, which in some details no longer quite fits the modified English version reprinted above. Ritter, however, is less concerned with making a point-by-point criticism than in stressing the inaccuracies of interpretation and emphasis, and thus to bring out by means of illustrations the importance of approaching the sources with understanding of their meanings within their proper contexts.*

It is part of Fischer's basic thesis that the German government, instead of seeking peace, actually considered war as necessary (in view of the development in the ratios of military strength) and saw in the July crisis of 1914 an especially favorable opportunity for a "great diplomatic success" which would push Russia completely out of the Balkans.

From Gerhard Ritter, "Eine neue Kriegsschuldthese?" *Historische Zeitschrift,* v. 194 (June 1962), pp. 657–668. Translated by D. E. Lee and Stewart A. Stehlin. Footnotes omitted.

But was our goal really this rather than the maintenance of our Austrian ally as a great power? In other words, is the German policy of 1914 to be understood as aggressive or defensive? Around that question in the final analysis revolved the vast controversy of historians of all countries, which since 1919 has brought to light mountains of documentary sources and monographs and which Fischer again revives. Nothing can be more troublesome and more unpleasant than to argue with him—just when one, like myself, is convinced that the older German war-guilt literature of the twenties and thirties has proved to be all too apologetic and in need of some revision. For a problem so difficult, so over-discussed, and so over-laden with source materials as the war-guilt question requires endless patience and conscientious care in the analysis of documentary evidence. Nowhere is there less room for "thesis history" than here.

Fischer explains, moreover, that he did not want to treat the war-guilt question anew, yet in fact he has done that. Only he already knew beforehand what he had to prove and proceeded into the collections of documents without being too selective.

As the first state witness for the Berlin government he brings forward a journalist, not a diplomat, Viktor Naumann, who as early as July 1 tried to persuade the General Secretary of the Vienna foreign ministry, Count Hoyos, to press for the attack on Serbia and promised him to work in the same sense in Berlin. Naumann was only the representative of patriotic currents of opinion in Germany, but had heard in the foreign office through Councillor von Stumm that they were greatly worried there over the rapidly growing Russian armament, and he thought (apparently correctly) that it was permissible to conclude from this and similar expressions that in the foreign office "they no longer rejected quite so completely the idea of a preventive war against Russia as they had a year before." That is really all there was to the matter. But the journalist attached to this idea political considerations concerning the necessity of risking even a European war because of Serbia, for which the Dual Alliance "was now still strong enough." That was grist for County Hoyos' mill, truly the least hesitant of all the Austrian warmongers, who then reported this conversation in detail to his minister. Fischer finds the conversation of "great significance," since Naumann's predictions were to be accurately confirmed by Germany's conduct in the July crisis. In fact they correspond accurately with the Fischer thesis. Are they, however, proof that the chancellor and the chief of the general staff wanted to unloose a preventive war?

The relation of the two allies is so portrayed by Fischer that Austrian policy was fundamentally peacefully oriented, and only through the greatest pressure by Berlin did Austria allow herself to be pushed into war. The Sarajevo assassination, so goes the account, was received in Austria with conflicting emotions, in part even with relief that the Slavophil heir to the throne had at last gone. Only a group around General Conrad had wanted to "settle accounts" with Serbia, but they were also hesitant. In contrast, from July 6, German policy, submitting without opposition to the monarchical opinions of Emperor William, pressed, not without threats concerning future alliance relations, for the strongest action even to the point of war. Now there is certainly no doubt that in Vienna they were anxious and uncertain so long as they had not made sure (through a special mission of Count Hoyos) that the German government was ready, just as in 1908 and differently than in 1912, to cover its ally in case of a conflict with Russia. From that, however, one cannot say that the initiative for the "settlement" with Serbia was forced upon the Austrians half violently by Berlin. It was they who requested support in Berlin, not vice-versa; and it means putting the course of events upside down when Fischer tries to ascribe responsibility to the German instead of the Austrian government for its disastrous diplomacy—and strategy—as lame as it was frivolous and insincere in the decisive weeks.

He obviously cannot—or will not—comprehend what the true motive was for the many Berlin admonitions advising Austria to take quick and energetic action. It was not a burning eagerness for war of some kind of militarist, but rather the very well-justified fear of the dilatory half-measures of the Austrians who left their opponents time for diplomatic and military counter-measures and thereby destroyed not only the political and moral impression of the Sarajevo outrage but also the practical success of every undertaking against Serbia. Granted that German policy in the July crisis relied upon false speculation. Indeed, it had falsely evaluated almost all factors: underestimated the war preparedness of Russia and France, overestimated the impression of the outrage upon the courts of Europe and the peacefulness of English policy, and, not least, far overvalued the military capacity, political wisdom and manageability of the Austrian ally. One can even ask after that whether their basic assumption had not been faulty; whether the maintenance of the Danubian empire as a great power was still worth such a huge risk; yes, whether it was even possible in the long run, and whether this ally basically was not more trouble to us than it was worth. But the historian who asks such questions will still be aware that he therewith completely departs from a historical understanding of that period; that is, that a German statesman of 1914 could not possibly ask such questions simply because he would have compromised himself in the eyes of the German as well as the Austrian peoples. He would appear not only as a treaty-breaker, as a cowardly weakling, but even as a traitor to the German cause. For the division of 1866 had still not divided the German nation so deeply that in imperial Germany they could look with equanimity upon the ruin of the "brother empire" (whose maintenance even Bismarck had always declared a European necessity); quite apart from the fact that at this period still they considered a Russian-dominated Balkans, including Hungary, as an unbearable threat to Central Europe. Thus, even Prince Lichnowsky, our London ambassador and the sharpest critic of the Berlin government's policy, explained in a private letter to Jagow that the idea of sacrificing Austria as an ally was farthest from his mind, but he did take the view that a military "punishment" of Serbia was a thoughtless folly of Viennese policy. Today we can see that he had hit the nail on the head, that a swift military destruction of Serbia could not have solved satisfactorily the irremediable nationality problem of the Danubian monarchy, especially since their statesmen were neither united nor completely clear about what they should actually do with such a victory. At the time they believed a rapid military triumph, as a "proof of power," would strengthen once more the greatly lowered esteem of the Danubian monarchy and constrain the small Slavic neighbor folk, at least for some time. If the monarchy, however, let the Sarajevo murder, the strongest of all provocations, pass without doing anything, then its rapid decline would no longer be delayed.

But if such a powerful stroke seemed to both governments to be necessary, then the blow must fall immediately without long negotiations with other powers, and before the impression of the bloody deed at Sarajevo had evaporated throughout the world. And thus, for Berlin, it was the most terrible disappointment when little by little it turned out that the Imperial and Royal army was not in fact able to do that, not even after detailed preparations which dragged out finally until August 12—and then denuded the Galician border of troops which thereby left Germany completely alone on the Russian front. Thus, then, the impression of almost all remarks of responsible German officials in the July weeks is that of a permanently growing and ever more severely oppressive anxiety. To overlook that and to discover some kind of desire for battle and confidence of victory is only possible with the help of radical and round-about interpretations.

One of the most curious examples of this kind of interpretation is the assertion that Under-Secretary of State Zimmermann on July 5 had "given Count Hoyos to understand" that Germany, in case of a Russian-French intervention, was able alone, because of its military position, to take on both, so that Austria-Hungary could concentrate entirely on the Balkans. To credit Zimmermann with such stupidity is to under-rate his intelligence considerably; there is not the slightest support for it in the sources. And does Fischer seriously believe that Prime Minister Count Stürgkh's anxiety that Austria would lose Germany's support in the future through feeble hesitation "refutes" the view presented from previous research that we intervened on behalf of the Danubian monarch in order not to sacrifice the last important ally?

Like the attitude of the German politicians, that of the leading military men is put entirely in a wrong light. Moltke is said to have spoken out in his last Karlsbad conversation with Conrad von Hötzendorf for a "speedy attack" and therefore had shown himself resolutely in favor of war. Not a word about that exists in the sources. In truth the discussion was extremely serious in tone: they agreed fundamentally on how uncertain the prospects of success had become because of the defection of Rumania and the powerful preparations of Russia. Moltke was certainly greatly distressed by the prospect of Russia surpassing us in armaments even further in the coming years ... so that "every delay meant the lessening of the chances"—a worry which he appears to have expressed many times in the summer of 1914. Fischer has completely ignored my proof that these may not be taken as eagerness for war. He appears to find somehow as striking the harmless communication of the Quartermaster General Waldersee to Jagow that he would remain quietly in his health resort, for the general staff was certainly "ready" (namely with its deployment plans and preparations for mobilization that were routinely drawn up anew every spring), for Fischer calls attention to the words "ready" and "prepared." On the same level is his interpretation of a letter in which Bethmann Hollweg, on July 16, asked the State Secretary of Alsace, Count Roedern, to prevent possible Francophobe remarks by the Alsatian press; French chauvinism was not to be provoked just now, since everything depended upon the localization of the Austro-Serbian conflict. From this Fischer inferred that "the break-up of the Entente, the chief objective of pre-war diplomacy, Bethmann Hollweg now thought to force through at any price—with or without war." Can one argue any more one-sidedly?

It is peevish to cavil over such details; but it is unavoidable, for in their accumulation they distort the picture of the reality unrecognizably for the not-well-enough-informed reader—and always unfavorably for Germany. Fischer's book reports something about two dispatches of Lichnowsky from London on July 27, from which Grey's deep-seated ill-feeling over the German attitude became perceptible for the first time. Bethmann had communicated the first of these, which reported the ambassador's discussion with Sir Edward, to Vienna and also to the Kaiser on the very same day (for Fischer, however, the telegram is belated, namely by seven hours), and was a serious warning to Berchtold not simply to reject the English proposals. But Fischer tells of that warning only two pages later in another context, and immediately reports that the second telegram of Lichnowsky's, which contained only his personal opinion, was not circulated, so that the reader who is not informed inevitably gets the impression (and is angered by it) that the serious warning from London had simply been put in the files.

Now today it will surely occur to no one to find the attitude of Bethmann and Jagow toward the English warning politically wise and right. That up to July 29 they did not take it seriously enough and held firmly too long to the idea that they should not fail their ally and spoil for it the (apparently last) chance to establish its prestige again through a speedy military success, was a miscalculation that almost bordered on delusion. Why must the critic, however, be overcome by this mistake, while he continuously talks of intentional delay if a London dispatch was debated a few hours in Berlin before being sent to Vienna, and of "suppression" of the truth, or, indeed of "falsification" if a sentence merely intended for Berlin was left out as well? Above all, why does Fischer try to exonerate the crafty policy of a Berchtold, as vacillating as it was flippant, to the disadvantage of Bethmann? I myself must repeat that I want to refute again the assertion (stemming from Albertini) that officials in Vienna after July 14 had "let it be known that they did not want it to come to extremes" and that only because of the forceful pressure from Berlin was Vienna led to its precipitate declaration of war, which was to end all attempts of the great powers at mediation. Fischer even sees the fact that Bethmann's most urgent admonitions to come to an agreement with Russia took place only on the evening of the 29th as proof that Austro-Hungarian policy "throughout was not tough and stubborn" and that in Vienna up to the 29th/30th they had not been seriously restrained, but had always been pushed forward. As proof of that he uses those additions to the Berlin telegrams in which our ambassador Tschirschky was instructed, in transmitting the London proposals "to avoid the impression that we wish to hold Vienna back," in pursuit of its goals of conclusively cutting the vital cord of the Greater Serbia propaganda, but everything had to be done to reach this goal without war, and if that should not be possible, "to improve the conditions under which we shall have to wage it, insofar as is possible."

Fischer interprets these additions as if they had intentionally pursued the objective of sabotaging the effect of the foregoing admonitions to be moderate and ready to negotiate—a very peculiar kind of diplomacy! The possibility that the additions were intended to spare the sensitivity and mistrust of the Vienna government (which always so easily felt itself patronized) and to make its compliance somehow more palatable is not once considered. For our author once for all firmly holds that Bethmann definitely did not want peace because he believed that he was obliged not to shun war, and he had now decided upon "a great diplomatic success" for Germany. The protestations of his love for peace were pure hypocrisy and likewise the warnings to Vienna were intended exclusively to push the responsibility for the war onto the Russians, whose need for prestige Fischer evidently finds to be as justified as that of the Central Powers was unjustified. Already the fact that the imperial chancellor had always emphasized in Vienna that Germany and Austria dare not appear before the world and before their own people as aggressors and as guilty of war is to him most highly suspicious; Bethmann therefore depended only upon the appearance of peace, not upon peace as such.

Up to the night of July 29/30, he had sought to deceive England through this appearance and to influence her toward neutrality—although as early as the 27th Grey had "seen through the German game." And yet in the conversation with British Ambassador Goschen, in the late evening of the 29th, Bethmann had appeared as "almost sure of victory, yes, high handed"; he had even now "revealed his goal" to the Englishman: "the first steps of German war aims, which soon after the outbreak of war appeared clearly," were the overthrow of France and Belgium, the acquisition of French colonies as a continuation of the Morocco policy of 1911, and so forth. What inconceivable folly, the reader will be compelled to say, when he learns that Bethmann Hollweg had sought to win England's consent to such plans. All the more dramatic was the effect of the sudden breakdown of all hopes of British neutrality that same night when Lichnowsky's report arrived that Grey had told him England could not remain neutral in case of a Franco-German war. But tough as ever, the chancellor held firmly to his fictions. No longer for the sake of England but for that of German Social Democracy he now rushes his last pressing admonitions and warning to Vienna (2:55 and 3:00 a.m.). The innocence of Germany and Austria must be demonstrated! It was only for that reason that he struggled so stubbornly and long against the demands of the chief of the general staff and of the war minister to answer in time the Russian mobilization, already begun, with a German counter-mobilization; the Russian total mobilization should first be awaited—for the sake of appearances! Proof of the domestic political motive (the Social Democrats) was Bethmann's remark in a meeting of the Prussian cabinet on July 30 that he believed he could rely on the loyalty of the Social Democrats in case war broke out.

Thus the impression of the chancellor's efforts (too late, to be sure) to put the brakes on the Viennese war policy even at the last moment is reduced to nothing. For that purpose, however, yet a further, almost more grotesque proof is made to serve and is emphatically underlined by our author: Bethmann cancelled his dispatch to Vienna on the evening of July 30, about nine o'clock, which contained a new, quite unequivocal admonition to come to an understanding with Russia, by a new telegram at 11:20 p.m., because at 11:08 (!) a rather unimportant dispatch from the King of England to Prince Henry had arrived which appeared to offer a new "glimmer of hope" for English neutrality—and therefore made stopping the war unnecessary!

Does not Fischer know the true reason, namely that significant conference of the chancellor with Moltke and Falkenhayn on the late evening of July 30, the tragic turning point of the whole July crisis, in which the generals convinced the resisting chancellor that it was already too late for mediation attempts and negotiations with the Russians, since according to the information of the general staff Russian total mobilization was already obviously in progress? Their apprehensions were confirmed, moreover, in the course of the night. Nevertheless Fischer appears not to believe the genuineness of these reasons. Rather, he maintains offhandedly that an excited marginal note of the Emperor on a dispatch from Petersburg, which revealed Russian partial mobilization against Austria, had removed all the previous inhibitions . . . as if eagerness for war and not burning anxiety concerning the well-timed execution of the now rigidly fixed Schlieffen plan had prevailed at the general staff! Whoever reads the sources soberly and without bias can only shake his head at such a contrived interpretation.

Naturally the true reason for the nervous pressure of Moltke for the total mobilization of Austria on July 29/30 remains completely misunderstood—as completely misunderstood as in the older war-guilt literature up to Albertini. Fischer has taken no notice of my pains to clear up the military-technical relationships. Instead, he piles up fictitious arguments in order to read into the German policy of July motives of imperialistic power and conquest. . . .

Moltke's attitude immediately before the outbreak of the war is generally pictured in a way for which the expression "biased" seems to me altogether too mild. One knows that he fell into despair when the Emperor on the evening of August 1 suddenly ordered him to stop the war in the west, which had already begun, because a remarkable telegram (quickly recognized as an error) of Lichnowsky's for a moment rekindled the hope that England would guarantee French neutrality if we renounced the idea of attacking in the west. Moltke's excitement over this unexpected disruption of his plan and over the presumptuous demand of the Emperor to turn the whole deployment toward the east, I myself have characterized as a personality failing (similar to that of Falkenhayn and Tirpitz). But there can be no doubt at all about what gave rise to this excitement: the general staff did not believe, any more than the war minister did, that France would actually keep still and considered Lichnowsky's report (correctly so) as a soap bubble. Had Moltke followed the Emperor's command, it would only have led to awful chaos; besides Moltke got a most ungracious reception of his remonstrance by William II and the latter's just as careless as dilettantist interference in strategic decisions seemed to be evidence of distrust that deeply shocked him. No one who can read the sources impartially will understand his exclamation at this moment, "Now, it only remains for Russia to back out, too!" which was recorded by Admiral Müller (in a greatly shortened note), as anything other than bitter irony. Fischer, who asserts that the Chief of the General Staff was "beside himself over the possibility of a neutral France," suggests to the reader that he was just as frightened over a "backing out of Russia"—therefore frightened (what should one infer otherwise than that?) over the maintenance of peace.

After all that, it is hardly rewarding to argue with Fischer's concluding considerations concerning "who was guilty," in which he seeks to support his thesis by the later retrospective views of Tisza, Czernin, Admiral von Müller, Ballin, and Bethmann Hollweg, which he interprets as either a kind of confession of guilt, or as accusations by well-informed participants. He does not speak exactly of Germany's sole guilt, but says, cautiously and informally, that "the governments of the participating European powers in one way or another and in very different degrees shared in the responsibility for the outbreak of the World War." Since in his exposition, however, there is not a syllable about the co-responsibility of the non-German powers, it seems to me as good as excluded that any reader will interpret this background of the war as something other than a renewal of the guilt clause of Versailles. A completely new picture of Chancellor Bethmann Hollweg is put before us. In place of a very conscientious, honest, but in his decisions changeable official who was always beset by fresh doubts and was lacking in a sure political instinct, there appears a tough and crafty power-politician who plays with the fate of Germany with unscrupulous flippancy (one can hardly call it anything else). And this impression is accumulated massively throughout the main part of the book, and is strengthened by documents from the time of the World War, always interpreted in the same sense.

In summary, let it be said that this work for the first time has applied the thesis of Ludwig Dehio (which is as glittering as it is dangerous and is in the last analysis only a half-truth) concerning the "war for hegemony" as the essence of both world wars, in a great exposition from the sources. At the same time in Fischer a first peak is reached in today's fashionable stream of political history— the obscuring of Self in German historical consciousness that, since the catastrope of 1945, has superseded the earlier apotheosis of Self, and now appears successfully and one-sidedly to assert itself. I am convinced that it will work out not less fatefully than the superpatriotism of former times. Thus I lay the book down not without genuine sadness—sadness and anxiety respecting the coming generation.

Konrad H. Jarausch
BETHMANN HOLLWEG'S CALCULATED RISK

A member of the History Department at the University of Missouri, Konrad H. Jarausch has sought to reinterpret Chancellor Bethmann Hollweg's policy in the July crisis of 1914 in the light of previously unused primary sources. Since the appearance of the article reprinted below he has published a full-scale study entitled Bethmann Hollweg and the Hubris of Imperial Germany *(1973). How does his interpretation compare or contrast with that of George Peabody Gooch and of Fritz Fischer, which are reprinted above?*

The responsibility for the outbreak of World War I weighed heavily upon Imperial Germany's fifth Chancellor, Theobald von Bethmann

From Konrad H. Jarausch, "The Illusion of Limited War: Chancellor Bethmann Hollweg's Calculated Risk, July 1914," *Central European History*, II (1969): 48–50, 54–60, 64–76. Reprinted with the omission of footnotes by permission of *Central European History*.

Hollweg. "This war torments me," he confessed to the Liberal Conrad Haussmann during the struggle. "Again and again I ask if it could have been avoided and what I should have done differently." This soul searching led Bethmann to believe that "all nations are guilty; Germany, too, bears a large part of the blame." Arguing that "our fate is too colossal to have its origins in singular events," the Chancellor stressed the larger causes of the conflict. Imperialist rivalry, the anti-German coalition, the growing isolation of Berlin, and Vienna's relative decline, "all that forced us to adopt a *policy of utmost risk,* a risk that increased with each repetition, in the Moroccan quarrel, in the Bosnian crisis, and then again in the Moroccan question." But he also admitted candidly: "Lord yes, in a certain sense it was a preventive war," motivated by "the constant threat of attack, the greater likelihood of its inevitability in the future, and by the military's claim: today war is still possible without defeat, but not in two years! Yes, the generals," he repeated. "It could only have been avoided by a rapprochement with England, that is still my conviction. But after we had decided for a [common] policy with Austria, we could not desert her in such danger." Suspecting that "it borders on a preventive war," Bethmann silenced his conscience by denying that "we *encouraged* Austria to attack Serbia, which sounds as if we had taken the initiative. That is absolutely false."

For fifty years historians have endeavored to resolve the contradictions inherent in Bethmann's self-justification. Returned from the sword to the pen, Entente and German scholars attacked one another so violently that the ex-Chancellor cautioned in 1920: "The war-guilt question must be treated *objectively* by all. Any other method is suspect. The partisan polemics are beginning to nauseate the public." But his call for moderation went unheeded and during the interwar period the *Kriegsschuldfrage* became a symbolic focus of nationalist sentiments. The Second World War confirmed the verdict of Versailles, but in the early 1950s the questioning of nationalism produced a Franco-German declaration, assigning a share of the responsibility to all. More recently Fritz Fischer's rediscovery of Bethmann's annexationism reopened the old wounds, allowing East German and Western historians to affirm what they had long suspected: The war "was deliberately provoked, not stumbled into." Most West German scholars, led by Egmont Zechlin, rallied behind their dean, the late Gerhard Ritter, claiming in spiritual defense of their fatherland that it was not a preventive but a defensive war. Now historians must once more face the perennial question. Did Germany unleash the war deliberately to become a world power or did she support Austria merely to defend her weakening ally?

Curiously enough, one of the obvious avenues of investigation has hitherto been neglected: the study of Germany's constitutionally re-sponsible statesman, Chancellor Bethmann Hollweg. A fascinating new document, the diary of his personal *adlatus* in the *Wilhelm-strasse,* Kurt Riezler, offers fresh perspectives on the motives of Bethmann's policies in the July crisis. Scion of a family of prominent South German scholars, Riezler worked as a freelance writer after completing his doctorate and entered the imperial foreign service in 1909. Three years later this gifted and spirited young man was detailed to serve as Bethmann's special assistant, drafting directives and helping to shape and clarify policy. To systematize his expe-rience Riezler wrote two books on world politics before 1914, arguing for the necessity of a unified theory of international relations and sketching the general outlines of German *Weltpolitik.* Source of ideas, partner for thought-provoking discussions, and confidant of the Chancellor, he lacked any firm place in the governmental hier-archy. Hence his diary is an artistic record of moods, feelings, and conversations, rather than a systematic exposition of fact; but pre-cisely its intuitive quality helps resolve the enigma of Bethmann's aims in the July crisis.

*   *   *

The initial response of the German government to the assassina-tion [at Sarajevo] was hesitant, groping, and generally peaceful. Old Count Tschirschky, German ambassador to the Hofburg, affirmed Berlin's support of the alliance, but "used every opportunity in order to warn quietly but seriously and emphatically against precipitous steps." Remembering Franz Ferdinand's warm hospitality only three weeks earlier, the impetuous Emperor called for a showdown with Serbia "now or never," reprimanding the ambassador for his timid-ity. Count Tschirschky must have heard of the royal displeasure since he assured Francis Joseph several days later "that Germany would firmly back Austria, if its vital interests were imperiled." The envoy's emphasis on a concerted plan of action foreshadowed a firmer German stand, but the Chancellor was still vacationing at Hohenfinow and Foreign Secretary Jagow was on his honeymoon.

On July 5, William II recalled Bethmann to Berlin to consider Francis Joseph's appeal for help, transmitted by the hawkish Austrian diplomat Count Hoyos. "The Emperor received me and Undersecretary of State Zimmermann in the Park of the *Neues Palais* in Potsdam. No one else was present," the Chancellor later recalled. Having read the strongly worded Austrian memorandum, "the Emperor declared that he could not deceive himself about the grave danger in which the pan-Serbian propaganda had place Austria. But it was not up to us to advise our ally how to react to the bloodbath of Sarajevo. Vienna herself had to decide that." William recommended a three-fold response: "We should abstain from direct influence and advice, since we should work with all our means towards the goal of not letting the Austro-Serbian quarrel become an international conflict." But "Emperor Francis Joseph should know that we will not desert Austria-Hungary in this serious hour. Our own vital interests demand the preservation of Austria" as a great power. And following Berchtold's advice, "he considered it desirable to draw Bulgaria [into the alliance] as long as that would not alienate Rumania." Bethmann accepted this analysis since "these opinions of the Emperor coincided with my own." Later the same afternoon the hastily recalled military advisers of William minimized the gravity of the expected risk. Summarizing the informal discussions between Bethmann, Zimmermann, Minister of War Falkenhayn, and the chief of the military cabinet Lyncker, Adjutant General Plessen jotted into his diary: "The opinion prevails that we should move against Serbia *the sooner the better,* and that the Russians—although friends of Serbia—will not intervene." But Falkenhayn reassured Moltke, Chief of the General Staff: "The Chancellor, who was also in Potsdam, seems to believe as little as I that the Austrian government is serious about its recently more forceful language."

With such military encouragement, Bethmann gave the Austrian ambassador, Count Szögyény, one of the most momentous assurances of European history the following morning: "Concerning Austria's relations with Serbia the German government believes that Vienna has to judge what has to be done to clarify this relationship; in this undertaking it can count safely on Germany's support of the monarchy as ally and friend—whatever its decision." To bolster the war party in Vienna, Szögyény concluded his dispatch energetically: "In the further course of the conversation, I realized that the Chancellor, like his imperial master, considers our immediate intervention against Serbia the most radical and the best solution of our Balkan difficulties."

Why did Bethmann Hollweg depart so suddenly and fundamentally from his earlier policy of restraint towards Austria during the Balkan wars? The official documents contain no clue to his motivation. Conscious of Berchtold's desire for local war, the Chancellor gave more than a blank check. Prodded by William, Hoyos, and Zimmermann and encouraged by the generals, Bethmann formulated a coherent rationale, calling for a diplomatic offensive on the Balkans in which the Austrian punishment of Serbia would be just one part. Contrary to the tenor of the alliance with Rumania, Bethmann informed his ambassador in Bucharest that "H. M. understands that Emperor Francis Joseph considers reconciliation with Serbia impossible and attempts to counteract the dangers threatening his House and Empire from Belgrade through an alliance with Bulgaria." The Sarajevo assassination gave Germany the historic chance for breaking the tightening vise of encirclement through a realignment of the southeastern powers. The adherence of Bulgaria and Turkey to the Triple Alliance and the strengthening of dynastic ties with Rumania and Greece would isolate Serbia politically and militarily and eliminate Russian influence from the area. A quick diplomatic or if need be military triumph of Austria would restore the Central Powers' waning prestige. When the *Frankfurter Zeitung* predicted on July 9 that Vienna's "diplomatic and political action" against Belgrade would "probably be executed in *short, swift strokes,*" Bethmann heartily agreed: "Very good."

Back in Hohenfinow after the momentous decision, the Chancellor explained the reasons for his reversal to Riezler "at night on the veranda under the starry sky." Bethmann pessimistically regarded the rumored "Anglo-Russian negotiations for a naval agreement and a landing in Pomerania as the last link in a chain." Although the British Admiralty publicly denied these reports, the increasing military cooperation among the Entente distressed the Chancellor. Bethmann feared that the German ambassador to the Court of St. James, Prince Lichnowsky, was much too credulous and could easily be duped by the wily British. Recent general staff studies had reinforced

Bethmann's fear of "Russia's quickly growing military might. After the completion of their strategic railroads in Poland our position [will be] untenable." Austria was growing "weaker and more immobile" by the day. Vienna was "increasingly undermined from north and southeast, at any rate incapable of going to war for German interests as our ally." The Chancellor dismally concluded his military assessment: "The Entente knows that we are, therefore, completely paralyzed."

The crime of Sarajevo called for "grave decisions." Apparently "official Serbia [is] incriminated. Austria wants to pull itself together," judging from "Francis Joseph's mission to the Emperor inquiring about the *casus foederis.*" Now the Chancellor was confronted with our "old dilemma at every Austrian action in the Balkans. If we encourage them, they say we pushed them into it. If we discourage them, they say we left them in the lurch." Despairingly he predicted: "Then they will throw themselves into the open arms of the Western powers and we lose our last important ally." Fearing the break-up of the Dual Alliance, strained by German moderation in the Balkan wars, Bethmann considered his predicament "worse than in 1912, because this time Austria is on the defensive against Serbo-Russian intrigues" and could not be restrained so easily. Backing Vienna entailed considerable risks as well: "An attack on Serbia can lead to world war." Any general conflagration "however it ends [will lead] to a revolution of all existing conditions." But inaction was worse: "The future belongs to Russia which grows and grows, looming above us as an increasingly terrifying nightmare." Under this heavy responsibility Bethmann decided on a leap forward. "Perhaps the old Emperor [Francis Joseph] will prefer not to fight after all," the Chancellor consoled himself. "If war comes from the east so that we have to fight for Austria-Hungary and not Austria-Hungary for us, we have a chance of winning." And better yet, "if war does not break out, if the Tsar is unwilling or France, alarmed, counsels peace, we have the prospect of splitting the Entente."

Although uncertain about the likelihood of war, Bethmann resolved to run a calculated risk. Full support of Berchtold's desire for the punishment of Serbia could have three consequences: A local Balkan war would bring a diplomatic triumph, a realignment of the southeastern states and the break-up of the Entente. Equally likely seemed a continental war, engulfing Russia, Austria, France, and

Germany. In such a conflict, the general staff promised a good chance of winning. Less desirable than a localized conflict, a continental struggle might ease the Russian pressure from the east, revitalize faltering Austria and regain the diplomatic initiative in the Balkans. In Bethmann's mind only the last alternative was fraught with unacceptable danger: world war. The intervention of Britain or any other great power would upset the carefully balanced odds. Bethmann did not gamble frivolously, but because he considered "our position desperate," hoping only, "if war comes and the veils fall, the whole nation will follow, driven by necessity and peril." Riezler longed for "victory as liberation," since he was "too young not to succumb to the lure of the new, the great movement." But for Bethmann "this action is a leap in the dark and as such the most serious duty." While the pan-Germans were jubilant, the navy, army, and colonial leagues ecstatic, and the students feverish with misguided idealism, the aging Chancellor entered on the uncertain course with great reluctance.

Bethmann's diplomatic gamble was not only endorsed but actively promoted by the other leaders of the Wilhelmian empire. The Emperor's early pro-war commitment prejudiced the issue before his Chancellor could advise differently. In the absence of the cautious Jagow, the energetic Zimmermann was swayed by Hoyos who considered the moment opportune for a *Rachezug* against Serbia, and when summarizing the Austrian memorandum Zimmermann counseled Bethmann to take resolute action. Only two months earlier Moltke had told Jagow: "We must wage a preventive war to conquer our opponents as long as we still have a reasonable chance in the struggle." The emotional impact of the murder on the sincere monarchist Bethmann at a time when he was still in mourning over the death of his wife was also severe. But there is no proof of industrialist pressure for war. On the contrary, English Ambassador Goschen stressed in a private letter to Sir Arthur Nicolson in London: "I hear in fact from all sides that the financial and industrial classes are dead against a war in any shape—but particularly against a war which in its origins does not touch German interests." In the July crisis of 1914 Bethmann believed that he acted in keeping with his earlier rejected letter of resignation in protest against the naval race: "If war is forced upon us, we shall fight and, with God's help, not perish. But to conjure up a war ourselves without having our honor or vital interests imperiled, this I would consider a sin against Germany's destiny, even if human foresight would predict a total victory." . . .

On July 26, William II decided to return with the German fleet, contrary to his Chancellor's urgent advice. The Emperor feared another Port Arthur and curtly ordered Bethmann to report to him on the situation the following afternoon in Potsdam. But the Chancellor replied: "As long as Russia does not commit a hostile act, I believe that our stand, directed towards *localization,* must *remain* peaceful, too." First rumors of Russian mobilization spurred Bethmann to warn Lichnowsky: "Should they be confirmed, we would be forced to take counter-measures against our will. Even today we try to localize the conflict and keep peace in Europe. We therefore ask Sir Edward Grey [the British Foreign Minister] to use his influence in Petersburg in this direction." Bavarian Ambassador Lerchenfeld believed that "the policy of the German Empire is directed towards having our ally [Austria] emerge with a gain in prestige but also towards maintaining world peace." The goal of a Balkan victory but prevention of a general war inspired the Chancellor's instruction to Ambassador Schoen in Paris: "We cannot mediate in the conflict between Austria and Serbia, but probably [we will do so] between Austria and Russia."

The initial reaction of the great powers to the ultimatum was not too discouraging. "It is of crucial importance that Sazonov, though angry, has avoided committing himself. Paris is aghast at England's cold shoulder: an Austro-Serbian conflict does not concern me. Italy blackmails. [Vienna and Rome] have apparently not yet agreed. Everything depends upon Petersburg, will it mobilize immediately and be encouraged or discouraged by the West?" Now Bethmann grew pessimistic about the outcome: "The Chancellor sees a fate greater than human power hanging over Europe and our nation." His dark forebodings were brushed away by the reaction of the people, milling around the *Wilhelmstrasse:* "At first the Chancellor thought only young men would delight in the opportunity for ruckus and excitement and parade their curiosity. But the crowds grew and grew, the songs rang truer, the Chancellor was finally deeply moved, touched and heartened, since similar news poured in from all corners of the Empire." Riezler saw "an immense, if undirected drive for action in the people, a longing for great movement, for supporting a noble cause, for showing one's valor." A shy and retiring man, Bethmann was deeply moved by this wave of sympathy, which seemed to vindicate his perilous course.

While the Chancellor supported mediation between Vienna and Petersburg, Grey suddenly jeopardized the essential precondition of his strategy: "England's language has changed—apparently London finally realized that the Entente will be torn asunder if Whitehall is too luke-warm towards Russia. Lichnowsky has completely lost his composure." Bethmann feared the grave "danger that France and England will commit their support to Russia in order not to alienate it, perhaps without really believing that for us mobilization means war, thinking of it as a bluff which they answer with a counterbluff." Grey's declaration that he could no longer keep Britain aloof from the Austro-Serbian quarrel rendered localization impossible, since no one was left to mediate between the alliances. "As long as it remained Austro-Serbian" the British Foreign Secretary "would hold back. But now Grey sees himself forced to intervene, since the conflict threatens to become Austro-Russian and thereby European." Although never completely sure of British neutrality, Bethmann had based his decision for a diplomatic offensive on the assumption of England's cooperation in limiting the spread of a Balkan conflict, as in 1913. Now Grey's change in position, endangering localization, created "immense commotion in the *Wilhelmstrasse*. Nobody sleeps. I [Riezler] see the Chancellor only for seconds." The sudden danger transformed him completely. "He has not a minute to ponder and is fresh, active, lively, and without anxiety."

Although on the day of the Austrian declaration of war the situation improved temporarily, Bethmann was becoming disgusted with his ally, since Vienna's hesitation increased the likelihood of English interference. "This Austrian ambiguity is unbearable. They refuse to inform us of their program, saying *expressis verbis* that Count Hoyos' suggestion to partition Serbia was purely private; in Petersburg they act like lambs, thinking no evil; and in London their embassy boasts about doling out Serbian territories to Bulgaria and Albania." The Chancellor was desperately trying to control the crisis according to his original plan. Bethmann instructed Pourtalès to emphasize Vienna's denial of territorial interests in Serbia to Sazonov in order to keep Russia from mobilizing, while Lichnowsky should stress in London that the conflict was not between the alliances but merely between two Balkan powers. Simultaneously he was pressing the diplomatic offensive in Sofia and Constantinople to be in a better position, should a wider conflict arise.

On reading Serbia's conciliatory reply to the ultimatum, William II suddenly reversed his bellicose stand, deciding that Vienna should be content with a diplomatic triumph. This was a clear defection from the original strategy, which had considered a diplomatic victory insufficient, because of the internal malaise of the Habsburg monarchy. Bethmann accommodated himself to the imperial *volte face* by communicating the British offer of mediation to Tschirschky, without endorsing it so as not to embarrass Berchtold. In the early morning hours of the following day the Chancellor instructed his ambassador to transmit the "Halt in Belgrade" scheme to Francis Joseph as a peaceful alternative or as an alibi, should everything fail. "It is of utmost necessity that the responsibility for the expansion of the conflict to the other powers should, in all circumstances, fall upon Russia." Despite the Austrian declaration of war, Bethmann hoped that British mediation would prevent the spread of the conflagration, as long as Vienna quickly seized Belgrade from Serbia and then negotiated with St. Petersburg before the latter could mobilize.

The full effect of the Austrian declaration of war was felt only on the afternoon of July 29. By collaborating closely with Sir Edward Grey, Bethmann hoped to prevent Russian mobilization. In repeated conversations with Goschen and in numerous instructions to Lichnowsky, he tried to localize the conflict, while criticizing Grey's proposal for a conference of Ambassadors to mediate in the dispute, because it would mean a new Algeciras for Germany. His difficulties increased when later the same day the news of partial Russian mobilization reached Berlin: "Now we had to work at top speed for five days in a row from five or six in the morning," Riezler complained. Russian pressure forced Bethmann to decide "to what extent Germany should meet the English proposal of mediation." Serious disagreements developed between the *Wilhelmstrasse* and Prince Lichnowsky, making it all the more difficult for the Chancellor to communicate with Grey. Moreover "it was clear from the very beginning that Italy would not go along. They twist and turn the alliance treaty and [Foreign Minister] San Giuliano claims not to have been informed in time."

"Thank God, the Chancellor stepped in firmly," Riezler sighed in relief over the treatment of the Social Democrats. "Of course, there are generals who want to meddle immediately and shoot in order to 'teach the Reds a lesson.'" Over military protests, Bethmann succeeded in preventing the arrest of any Socialist leaders. "The Chancellor negotiated secretly with Südekum," a revisionist Reichstag deputy. In an unprecedented move, Bethmann drew a leading Socialist into his confidence with a candid assessment of the international situation. Later the same day Südekum answered for his party: "Your Excellency's step of directly informing [us] in this critical moment has met with full sympathy." Since Bethmann guaranteed that there would be no arrests, Südekum promised "that no action whatsoever (general or partial strike, sabotage, etc.) was planned or need be feared—especially because of our desire to serve peace." Because of this agreement the Chancellor exhorted the Emperor: "In all events Russia must ruthlessly be put into the wrong."

When the military leaders clamored for immediate mobilization, Bethmann countered that only if Russia mobilized first would England allow Germany to mobilize without intervening. For the time being Moltke and Falkenhayn acquiesced, but late that night they forced the Chancellor to send warnings to Petersburg and Paris to desist from further military preparations. Since British intervention was becoming more and more likely, Bethmann now seriously pressured Vienna to accept Grey's proffered hand by stopping in Belgrade. "We are certainly ready to fulfill our obligations as ally," he implored Berchtold, "but we clearly must refuse to be drawn lightly into a world conflagration by Vienna without consideration of our proposals." Riezler was even more disgusted with "the Austrians (bureaucrats gone mad, stubborn and dumb)" because of their reluctance in making territorial concessions to Rome in order to insure Italian neutrality. "All agree that if the *Ballplatz* had not procrastinated so long in its dealings with Rome and with the whole Serbian operation, everything would have ended in a diplomatic victory." Revealing the Chancellor's calculation, Riezler jotted down: "The Austrian action had to follow immediately . . . in the wake of the murder, not as a premeditated act, not as a long-prepared humiliation."

Grey's change of heart forced Bethmann to make a desperate move. Unable to achieve a clear picture of British intentions from the conflicting reports of Lichnowsky and the Hamburg shipping magnate Albert Ballin, the Chancellor decided to test Goschen with a formula reminiscent of the Haldane negotiations of 1912. "We can assure the English cabinet—*presupposing its neutrality*—" Bethmann beckoned, "that even in the case of a victorious war, we will seek no territorial aggrandizement in Europe at the cost of France." To assuage Whitehall's fear of a fundamental shift in the continental balance of power, the Chancellor declared that he would respect Dutch territorial integrity though leaving open the fate of the French colonies. "Presupposing that Belgium does not take sides against us," Bethmann was willing to guarantee its boundaries, but added: "We do not know which counter-measures French actions in a possible war might force us to take." His studied silence regarding Belgian sovereignty implicitly revealed the threat to its neutrality contained in Moltke's strategy of outflanking the French, following the Schlieffen Plan. But the Chancellor's purpose was diplomatic rather than military: "England's assurance of a neutral position in the present conflict," his most cherished goal, " 'would enable him [to enter into] a general neutrality agreement in the future,' " the reward of which—stricken on William's insistence—would be a naval agreement. On reading this "infamous" offer, the Germanophobe Crowe, Assistant to the Foreign Secretary, noted sarcastically: "The only comment that need be made on these astounding proposals is that they reflect discredit on the statesman who makes them." Though consistent with his earlier policy, Bethmann's blundering initiative was a desperate last-minute attempt to stave off British intervention with the crude promise of the territorial *status quo ante* in Western Europe, if London immobilized Paris, Brussels, and The Hague. British love for Berlin did not increase at gun-point and Jagow sourly conceded to Goschen the next morning that had Lichnowsky's warning of Grey's intention to keep his hands free arrived some hours earlier, Bethmann would not have taken this drastic step.

The 30th of July offered a respite to the harried Chancellor. Before the hastily assembled Prussian Ministry of State, Bethmann defended his strategy: *"Germany and England have undertaken all steps to avoid a European war."* Admitting that "we have lost control and the landslide has begun," he nevertheless insisted: "As a *political leader I am not abandoning my hope and my attempts to keep the peace* as long as my *démarche* in Vienna has not been rejected." More than ever before he pressed the *Ballplatz* to accept English mediation, but despite urgent long-distance calls, Berchtold refused any compromise. After a long internal struggle Russia now decided to mobilize. Frantic appeals to London and to Vienna to reestablish *pourparlers* with Sazonov were of little avail. The network of events had become too tangled to be unraveled without a major war. When the military demanded a deadline for the decision about mobilization, the reluctant Chancellor could do nothing but set it at noon on July 31. Explaining his predicament to Lerchenfeld, he claimed that he had done his utmost: "This evening I have most energetically declared to the Viennese cabinet that Germany will not swim in Austria's wake in the Balkans. Should Vienna reply affirmatively I still do not despair for peace." But Bethmann was too realistic to deny the danger: "Sad to say, through quasi-elemental forces and the persistent poisoning of relations among the cabinets, a war desired by no one might be unleashed."

When the news of the Russian general mobilization was confirmed at nine o'clock the next morning, the die was cast. "Strange that the unscrupulousness of the Russian grand dukes decided the issue in the enemy camp," Riezler mused four weeks later. "Perhaps they lied to the Tsar that Germany had already mobilized. At any rate they wildly exaggerated Russian strength, since they earn millions from war supplies." In deep sorrow he contrasted the "Chancellor's scruples" about his responsibility with the "icy hypocrisy" of Grey. Now Bethmann could no longer hold out against Moltke's demand for mobilization. An unauthorized telegram from the German Chief of Staff to General Conrad, his Austrian counterpart, snuffed out the last hope for moderation. Military necessity took over, the state of impending war was proclaimed, and ultimatums were sent to St. Petersburg and Paris.

The rest was anti-climactic. Bethmann and the Foreign Office went through the motions of last-minute compromise but they were directed more towards a closing of the ranks at home than towards peace abroad. A curious reversal had taken place. What had begun as a limited diplomatic offensive had passed beyond the bounds of politics into the realm of the military. Not personal weakness but the hallowed *Kommandogewalt* reduced the Chancellor to the position of being only one of several advisers to the Emperor. This Bis-

marckian legacy dimmed Bethmann's voice of restraint. The declarations of war against Russia and France, and especially the violation
of Belgian neutrality, were decided over his strongest protests. The
logic of his diplomatic gamble had carried Bethmann to the point
where he could only pray: "When the iron dice begin to roll, may
God help us!"

In this mood he took leave from the deeply agitated Goschen, who
exclaimed repeatedly: "Oh, it is too terrible!" Bethmann reminded
the British ambassador that it had been his foremost goal to establish closer relations with England: "All these attempts on which, as
he well knew, I had worked incessantly, were wrested from me. And
by whom? By England; and why? Because of Belgian neutrality!"
The Chancellor refused to believe that his work of five peaceful
years had been in vain: "Can this neutrality which we violate only
out of necessity, fighting for our very existence, and with the express
assurance that we will repay any damage, if Belgium lets us march
through—can this neutrality and the way in which it is threatened,
really provide the reason for a world war?" he queried. "Compared
to the disaster of such a holocaust does not the significance of this
neutrality dwindle into a scrap of paper?"

His entreaties, colored by remorse, came too late. Bethmann had
not accepted mediation soon enough. He had underestimated the
British commitment to the Entente, based on the strategic importance of the channel coast, and had failed to consider that his own
hand might be forced by the generals. Nevertheless, the Chancellor
passionately repeated: "It is a crime that Russia has forced war upon
us while we are still mediating between Vienna and Petersburg, and
a Franco-Russian war against Germany is enough of a disaster." The
calculated risk was leading to the third, most harmful alternative.
"This war turns into an unlimited world catastrophe only through
England's participation. It was in London's hands to curb French
revanchism and pan-Slav chauvinism. Whitehall has not done so, but
rather repeatedly egged them on. Now England actively helps them."
He protested movingly: "Germany, the Emperor, and the government
are peace-loving. That the ambassador knows as well as I do. We
enter the war with a clear conscience, but England's responsibility
is monumental." Sir Edward broke into tears. After a few moments,
the British ambassador regained his composure and left the chancellery.

Only in one respect did Bethmann's fears prove unfounded. The nation responded with great enthusiasm to what it considered a defensive war against Russia. "The incomparable storm unleashed in the people has swept before it all the doubting, half-hearted, and timid minds. The foreigners whom [Riezler] observed had tears in their eyes. The skeptical statesman was surprised by the nation." After the grave disappointment in England, this unexpected response from the people was heartening. Riezler well sensed "the uncontrived but profound effect of Bethmann's seriousness; the deep moral anguish from which every decision flows. Precisely that has called forth the best qualities of our inexhaustible nation." The upsurge of the masses, milling about Unter den Linden and singing *Heil Dir im Siegerkranz,* made Bethmann wax eloquent: "Should all our attempts [for peace] be in vain, should the sword be forced into our hand, we will go into battle with a clear conscience and the knowledge that we did not desire this war." But more candidly he sighed to Wahnschaffe, one of his closest friends, after signing the mobilization order: "It is a misfortune that I could not prevent the war. Now we must muster all our strength to win it."

The crucial decision of July 5 represents not the policy of one man, one class, or one branch of government; it was rather a tenuous compromise between the conflicting views of the decision-makers, Bethmann, William II, Zimmermann, Falkenhayn and the military entourage. According to the Saxon ambassador "the Foreign Office believes that war between Austria-Hungary and Serbia will be avoided." But the Emperor, deeply shocked by the assassination of Francis Ferdinand, reacted impulsively, demanding: "The Serbs have to be straightened out, and *soon!*" William II prejudiced the issue by assuring Szögyény and Hoyos his support before consulting the Chancellor, although reserving his final decision until Bethmann could approve. The military, represented by Prussian Minister of War Falkenhayn, chief of the military cabinet Lyncker, and Adjutant General Plessen, followed the imperial lead in pressing for strong punitive action. Aroused by Hoyos, Undersecretary of State Zimmermann and some of the younger officials of the *Wilhelmstrasse* also flirted with the use of force.

Under this pressure, the Chancellor embarked upon a political offensive in the Balkans in order to break the noose of encirclement. In November 1913 Bethmann had warned that pan-German dreams might turn into nightmares: "In any future war, undertaken without compelling cause, not only the Hohenzollern crown, but the future of Germany will be at stake. Certainly our policy must be led boldly," he admitted, "but to rattle the sword at every diplomatic entanglement without Germany's honor, safety, or future being threatened is not only blind, but criminal." His sudden resolve for action in July 1914 need not be attributed to fatalism or personal weakness. It rather resulted from the Chancellor's basic conviction that the pan-Slav agitation threatened the existence of Austria and thereby—according to Bismarck—Germany's vital interests. The Sarajevo assassination gave him the chance to reverse the deterioration of the Central Powers' diplomatic and military strength in one bold and dramatic stroke. Because of Europe's revulsion against the crime a swift punitive strike against Serbia could succeed without great power intervention. However, this initial compromise hardly decided anything at all. Vienna was still free to choose between diplomatic or military action, the generals could hope for the larger war, prepared so long, and the diplomats would strive unflaggingly to prevent the spread of the conflagration. Acceptance of the risk of local war and the possibility cf continental war—should it prove unavoidable—was the crucial shift in the Chancellor's policy which Szögyény reported to the *Ballplatz*: "Hitherto Bethmann has always advised us to get along with Serbia, but after the recent events, he realizes that it is well-nigh impossible."

If for three weeks Berlin spoke with a single voice, the precarious unity was shattered by two events: England's intervention and Russian mobilization. Torpedoing the strategy of localization, these unforeseen actions revealed a breach in the German leadership that made Berchtold utter in astonishment: "Who governs [in Berlin], Moltke or Bethmann?" Though he endorsed local war, the Chancellor watched the drift into continental war with growing apprehension and as soon as he realized the serious danger of world war, he desperately pushed for negotiations in Vienna while the generals grew more and more impatient to fight. "The Chancellor told me last night," Goschen cabled on the 30th, "that he was 'pressing the button' as hard as he could and that he was not sure whether [the] length to which he had gone in giving moderate advice in Vienna had not precipitated matters rather than otherwise." Fear of a general war was the motive behind the Chancellor's eagerness in seizing upon Lichnowsky's erroneous report that Britain might remain neutral after all. But the ambiguity of the original compromise had carried Bethmann to the brink of a world conflagration and transferred the final decision to the military. Only in this manner can the confusion of the *Wilhelmstrasse,* the consternation of the Chancellor and the complete lack of diplomatic preparation for war with France, Russia, and England be understood.

The strategy of localization was an act of desperation for Bethmann, a necessary risk to preserve the empire. Psychologically the German stand was, indeed, *defensive.* But the means that were adopted, the diplomatic offensive in the Balkans, the encouragement of Austrian punitive action against Serbia, the effort to prevent the intervention of the great powers and the attempt to split the Entente were *offensive.* Among the probable outcomes of the crisis Bethmann clearly preferred local war, was willing to gamble on continental war, but he abhorred world war. Believing that he had no alternative, the Chancellor decided on a "leap into the dark." As so often the concept of limited war proved elusive and drew Germany deeper and deeper into the vortex. Technically Austrian procrastination largely produced Grey's intervention and Russian mobilization. But after a generation of rampant imperialism, the risk of war could no longer be calculated in terms of cabinet diplomacy. Yet when reminiscing under the burden of defeat, Bethmann saw no other way. "We were severely handicapped by the war of [18]70–71 and by our geographical position. Since the coronation of Emperor [William II] we often did the opposite of that which would have lightened our burden," he admitted frankly. But "surely imperialism would have triumphed even without our help, and it remains highly questionable if, even with the most reasonable policy, we could have prevented the natural French, Russian, and English opposition from uniting against us. We have become guilty," he confessed, "but only universal and collective guilt has brought about the world catastrophe."

"I am no war chancellor!" Bethmann protested in deep anguish to Jagow when the bloodshed had become inescapable. "By God, we did not want this war," he repeated again and again to his moderate supporters at home and abroad. Though exaggerated, his recurrent claims contain a kernel of truth, because the Chancellor was drawn into the maelstrom of imperialism not as a rabid pan-German expansionist but as a traditional nationalist. Despite the

failure of his calculated risk, to Riezler "the Chancellor is the only
one who has gained new stature during the crisis. I have learned to
revere him because of his conduct, so self-effacing, self-denying,
and unostentatious. How silently he bears the burden of having to
lead the German people into war." In spite of his insistent dis-
claimers, the shadow of this responsibility pursued Bethmann to his
deathbed. During the height of the fighting he sighed to the liberal
journalist Theodor Wolff: "When assessing the responsibility for this
war—we have to confess honestly that we bear a share of the guilt.
If I said this thought oppresses me, I would say too little—this
thought never leaves me. I live in it."

III   NEW PERSPECTIVES ON THE OUTBREAK OF THE WAR

Arno J. Mayer
DOMESTIC CAUSES OF THE WAR

*Arno J. Mayer is professor of history at Princeton University. He has pub-
lished three books:* Political Origins of the New Diplomacy *(1959),* Politics
and Diplomacy of Peacemaking *(1967), and* The Dynamics of Counterrevolution *(1967). In the essay of which the first part is printed below, Professor
Mayer calls attention to the domestic tensions that accompanied the international tension in 1914, and suggests that in approaching the outbreak of
the First World War the historian should take account of the possible effect
of these internal disturbances upon the diplomatic decisions of the governments.*

When analyzing the origins of the Great War, diplomatic historians
continue to focus on two sets of underlying and precipitant causes:
those rooted in the dysfunctions of the international system and
those rooted in the mistakes, miscalculations, and vagaries of the
principal foreign policy actors. These historians assume that in a
multiple-state system the balancing of power is a natural and essential method of control, notwithstanding its inherent uncertainties. In
other words, they do not question or criticize the balancing-of-power
system or process as such. Instead, they tilt their lances at four
developments that complicated, if not obstructed, its smooth operation: (1) the alliance system, which became increasingly polarized
and rigidified, thereby threatening to transform any limited, local
conflict into an unlimited, general war; (2) the attendant armaments
race, which exacerbated mutual hostility, fear, and distrust; (3) the
new military metaphysics, which inclined civilian foreign-policy actors to become increasingly responsive to the military leaders and
their iron-clad timetables; and (4) public opinion, expressed and
mobilized through the daily press, notably the yellow and jingoist
dailies which were impatient with accommodation.

In addition to diagnosing these four dysfunctions in the balancing-of-power system or process, diplomatic historians also probe
into the personal attitudes, motives, and objectives of the principal

Arno J. Mayer, "Domestic Causes of the First World War," from *The Responsibility
of Power: Historical Essays in Honor of Hajo Holborn* by Leonard Krieger and Fritz
Stern, copyright © 1967 by Doubleday & Company, Inc., pp. 286–293. Reprinted by
permission of the publisher, with the omission of a footnote.

foreign-policy actors—heads of state, chief executives, foreign ministers, permanent foreign office officials, ambassadors, and military and naval officers. Not surprisingly, each major historian tends to have his favorite villain. Rather than indict entire nations, scholars tend to return verdicts against individual actors of a given nation or alliance. Three categories of charges are most commonly preferred: (1) that they made grave mistakes in diplomatic tactics; (2) that they miscalculated the responses of potential enemies; and (3) that they pursued objectives that were incompatible with the maintenance of the European equilibrium. But whatever the charge, in the last analysis their actions and judgments are said to have been warped by personal ambition, caprice, pique, or lack of backbone in the face of ruthless warmongers.

Admittedly, this framework of orthodox diplomatic history, tempered by amateur psychology, has been used to good advantage. It has served to uncover a great deal about the origins of the First World War in particular, and about the causes of international conflict in general.

Just the same, this time-honored approach has some rather grave limitations. In particular, it slides over (1) the proclivity of key foreign-policy actors to risk war in general, and preventive war in particular; (2) the degree to which they realized that any localized conflict was likely to develop into a major all-European or even world war; and (3) the extent to which they entertained recourse to external war for internal political purposes.

This third limitation stems very largely from the diplomatic historian's disposition to detach foreign policy hermetically from domestic politics; and to disconnect foreign-policy and diplomatic actors rigorously from the political and social context from which they originate and in which they operate.

Admittedly, this twofold dissociation, for analytic purposes, may not fatally handicap the study of the international politics of the relatively calm and elitist mid-eighteenth century. There seems little doubt, however, that this dual disjunction hinders the examination and understanding of foreign policy and diplomacy in such revolutionary eras as 1789 to 1815 and in such brief revolutionary spasms as 1848–1850.

This interconnection of domestic politics and foreign policy is exceptionally intense under prerevolutionary and revolutionary conditions. Characteristically, in the prewar years domestic tensions rose sharply at the same time that the international system became increasing strained. Moreover, this symbiotic growth of domestic and international tensions occurred in that part of the world in which, for the first time in recorded history, government policies, including foreign policies, were shaped in the crucible of organized party, pressure, and interest politics.

In other words, on the eve of war the major European polities were far from quiescent; and both the making and the conduct of foreign policy had ceased to be the private preserve of an encapsulated élite free of political pressures and neutral in the explosive domestic controversies of their respective societies. Accordingly, the 50 percent increase in military spending in the five prewar years may not have been exclusively a function of mounting international distrust, insecurity, and hostility. In some measure it may also have been a by-product of the resolve by conservatives and ultraconservatives to foster their political position by rallying the citizenry around the flag; and to reduce the politically unsettling cyclical fluctuations of the capitalist economies by raising armaments expenditures. In this same connection it should be stressed that the chief villains of July–August 1914—those foreign-policy actors whom diplomatic historians identify as having practiced reckless brinkmanship —were intimately tied in with those social, economic, and political strata that were battling either to maintain the domestic status quo or to steer an outright reactionary course.

To attenuate if not overcome the limitations of diplomatic history's conventional approach to the causes of war its analytic framework should be recast to accommodate three aspects of the historical and immediate crisis that conditioned and precipitated hostilities in July–August 1914: (1) the dysfunctions in the international system; (2) the domestic dysfunctions in the would-be belligerent nations; and (3) the inextricable interplay between these two sets of dysfunctions.

Whereas the dysfunctions in the international system and the diplomatic rivalries among the major powers have been studied exhaustively and are well-known, the same cannot be said about the prewar domestic dysfunctions, notably about their all-European scope.

During the decade, including the weeks immediately preceding

July–August 1914, the European nations experienced more than rou-
tine political and social disturbances. Even Britain, that paradigm
of ordered change and constitutionalism, was approaching the
threshold of civil war. Judging by the Curragh incident, Carson and
the Ulster volunteers had the sympathy if not outright cooperation
of influential civil and military leaders in their defiance of Parliament;
and the Triple Alliance of railwaymen, miners, and transport workers,
among whom militant syndicalists were ascendant, threatened a
paralyzing general strike in case their minimum demands were not
met by the fall of 1914. Whereas Ulster became the rallying issue and
symbol for an influential conglomeration of conservatives and reac-
tionaries, the strike project of the Triple Alliance roused extensive
support throughout the restless Labour movement. The resulting
polarization, along with the shift from debate in Westminster to direct
action in the streets, eroded the vital center so essential for the
politics of compromise and accommodation. Indeed, historians have
wondered whether if external war had not come in 1914 England
might not have become caught up in civil strife, with fatal damage
to her time-honored parliamentary system.

In France, meanwhile, the struggle between the right and the left
raged with unabated intensity around the twin issues of the three-
year draft and the progressive income tax. As in England, the center
of the political spectrum, which in France was multi-party in nature,
was being eroded in favor of the two opposing extremes. In particular, the left's strident antimilitarism, which the right construed as a
pressing social threat, frightened not only moderate republicans but
also radicals into a common political front with the right. In turn,
the *enragés* of the left made it increasingly difficult for the socialists
to cooperate with the center-left, which stood accused of truckling
to antirepublicanism. And, indeed, the right and center joined forces
in support of the three-year draft, capitalizing on the appeals of
nationalism to impugn the patriotism of the socialists, who advo-
cated a two-year draft. This reordering of political partnerships was
reflected in acute cabinet instability and in the antirepublican and
protofascist right becoming the backstop for a conservative-leaning
regime putting order and defense ahead of reform.

In Italy prewar political and labor disturbances culminated in the
explosive Red Week of early June 1914. Especially once this strike
wave subsided, and as usually happens in the wake of misfired

rebellions, the Italian middle-class nationalists assumed a position of intransigent hostility to the left—including the moderate left—which in 1915 took the form of taking Italy into the war against the will of the vast majority of the Italian nation.

As for Germany's semi-parliamentary system, which was the privileged preserve of conservative nationalists, it was heavily besieged by those parties—the Social Democrats, the *Zentrum*, the Progressives, and the moderate wing of the National Liberals—that denounced Prussia's three-class franchise and clamored for the cabinet's subordination to the Reichstag. Paradoxically, the mounting militancy in certain key trade unions scared off potential converts to political reform. In any case, according to Arthur Rosenberg, the political and social tensions in prewar Germany were "typical of a pre-revolutionary period," and if Germany had not gone to war in 1914 "the conflict between the Imperial Government and the majority of the German nation would have continued to intensify to a point at which a revolutionary situation would have been created."

The power élites in both halves of the Dual Monarchy faced increasingly explosive nationalistic unrest which, in itself, was an expression of spiraling political, economic, and social dysfunctions. Both Otto Bauer and Victor Bibl have argued convincingly that fear of southern Slav insurgency and of intensifying Austro-Czech tensions drove Vienna's political class into trying to overcome its permanent internal crisis by recourse to external war.

Simultaneously the Russian government, firmly controlled by unbending conservatives, confronted rising labor unrest in the major industrial centers alongside heightened restlessness among the peripheral national minorities. It was a sign of the times that during the first seven months of 1914 industrial unrest reached unparalleled scope and intensity, much of it politically and socially rather than economically motivated.

Great care must be taken to distinguish between, on the one hand, the actual scope and intensity of these internal tensions and disturbances, and, on the other hand, their perception, evaluation, and exploitation by the political contestants of the time. It is characteristic of prerevolutionary situations that hardened conservatives and counterrevolutionaries deliberately exaggerate all disorders, including the imminence of their transmutation into full-scale insurrection, in order to press and justify energetic precautionary measures. In turn, advanced reformers and revolutionaries similarly distort and distrust the intentions and actions of their domestic antagonists, charging them with preemptive counterrevolutionary design. But this mutual misrepresentation itself contributed to the polarization between the intransigent forces of order and the revolutionary forces of change, at the expense of the moderate, compromise-seeking center.

In Britain, France, and Italy parliamentary liberalism—the locus of this vital center—was heavily besieged, if not on the verge of collapse. The moderately reformist administrations of all three countries found it increasingly difficult to secure governing majorities. They were buffeted constantly by the parliamentary as well as extra-parliamentary pressures of the militant counterrevolutionary right and the militant revolutionary left. In Germany, Austria-Hungary, and Russia, where the ruling power élite considered even the advocates of integral parliamentarism dangerous revolutionaries, the vital center was almost completely emasculated.

It would seem that in these as in other prerevolutionary eras, the specter of revolution precipitated an active counterrevolutionary response among vulnerable status groups—the landed aristocracy, the petty nobility, the petite-bourgeoisie, the artisans, and the bypassed entrepreneurs. In fact, there may well be a certain parallelism between the attitudes and actions of such crisis strata in domestic politics and the attitudes and actions of foreign-policy actors who consider their nation's international power and prestige to be declining. In both instances the threatened parties are particularly prone to force a preemptive showdown—armed repression or insurrection at home or preventive war abroad—with the resolve of thereby arresting or reversing the course of history, which they claim to be turning against them.

Admittedly, much has been written about the antiwar agitation that was such a prominent aspect of the prewar thunder on the left. Considerably less is known about the superpatriotic agitation that was so central to the corresponding thunder on the right. To be sure, conventional diplomatic historians have noted the upsurge of nationalism before the war, and its further inflammation during and immediately following the July crisis. Few, however, have bothered to examine systematically the social, economic, and political background of the political organizers and social carriers of this nationalist revival. Surely it is not without significance that nearly all the superpatriots who clamored for preparedness and foreign-policy pugnacity held reactionary, ultraconservative, or protofascist views on domestic affairs. Before the war there were few if any liberal conservatives or reformers in the Navy League, the Tariff Reform League, and the pro-Entente wing of the Unionist and Liberal parties in England; in the *Action française,* the *Ligue des patriotes,* and the *Fédération des gauches* in France; in the Nationalist Party and the *fasci* in Italy; in the Pan-German League and the Conservative Party in Germany; in the war party centering around the Archduke in Austria-Hungary; and in the Assembly of the Russian People and the Black Hundreds in Russia.

Evidently foreign-policy issues became highly politicized, since notwithstanding governmental appeals, the primacy of foreign policy is inoperative under prerevolutionary conditions. Whereas the campaign against the arms race was an integral part of the struggle against the forces of order, the campaign for preparedness was a central feature of the struggle against the forces of change. All along the superpatriots of the two opposing camps did each other's bidding in that they exploited and fomented the mutual suspicion, fear, hostility and insecurity that quickened the European arms race. The Pan-German League and the *Action française* unwittingly helped each other at the expense of heightening international tensions. Domestically, meanwhile, they were instrumental in frightening liberal conservatives and reformists into supporting national preparedness, thereby eroding the vital center. In the parliamentary nations of Western Europe as well as in the autocratic empires of Central and Eastern Europe the prewar governments were particularly responsive to superpatriotic blandishments whenever moderate and advanced reformists threatened a united front, as was the case when Caillaux and Jaurès explored the basis for cooperation. In brief, the center increasingly relied on the right as a backstop, with the powerful encouragement of the upper echelons of the army, the foreign offices, the diplomatic corps, the ministry of the interior, and—in most cases—the church. Almost without exception these time-honored institutions were strongholds of the threatened and intransigent crisis strata rather than of the self-confident and supple business and banking grande-bourgeoisie.

To a not inconsiderable degree, then, throughout Europe the

rising international tensions were accompanied by rising internal tensions—by mounting social, political, and economic struggles that radicalized the extremes, eroded the center, and inclined the governments to push preparedness and diplomatic obduracy as part of their efforts to maintain a precarious domestic status quo. . . .

Joachim Remak
THE THIRD BALKAN WAR

Professor of history at the University of California, Santa Barbara, Joachim Remak has specialized in studying the backgrounds of World War I. He has published Sarajevo: The Story of a Political Murder *(1959), and a Berkshire Study entitled* The Origins of World War I, 1871–1914 *(1967). In the article reprinted below, he reviews the responsibility of the great powers and Serbia for bringing about the war, and concludes that everyone was "right" and everyone was "wrong." The temper of his approach to the problem is in striking contrast to that of Fischer, above, but Paul W. Schroeder, below, finds his exposition unsatisfactory.*

> *Everything the statesman creates is perishable, and in the long run, every decision is wrong. If it were otherwise, we would have no "history." [Golo Mann]*

Fritz Fischer's decade has ended. It began, neatly enough, in 1961 with *Der Griff nach der Weltmacht,* and drew to a close, in 1969, with *Krieg der Illusionen.* In between, there has been more discussion, scholarly and otherwise, than has been caused by any other single historian in our lifetime. Some of it has been stimulating. But the debate has just about run its course. Brecht's lines come to mind. I always hear Caesar did, Caesar conquered. Was not there at least a cook along?

From Joachim Remak, "1914—The Third Balkan War: Origins Reconsidered," *Journal of Modern History* 43 (1971): 353–366. Reprinted with the omission of footnotes by permission of the *Journal of Modern History* and the author.

*Phillipp von Spanien weinte, als seine Flotte
Untergegangen war. Weinte sonst niemand?*

Were not there some Frenchmen, too, in 1914, or some Serbians, who wept or laughed? A book that contains forty-five references in the index to Matthias Erzberger, and eighty to Karl Helfferich, and none to Sir Mark Sykes and none to Georges Picot, makes an interesting discussion guide but not a complete one. (This quite aside from the fact that the war's aims and origins were not always precisely identical.)

Where, though, if we cannot make Fischer's convictions or those of his partisans our own, does the responsibility for the First World War lie? What have the sixties taught us? Which statesmen, which nations, must bear the blame for war? To answer these questions, let us consider, in ascending order—and in the grand historical perspective which the drying of the blood and the passage of well over half of a century should provide—the responsibility of each of the belligerents.

This direct, national approach will be an old-fashioned one, but the exclusion of supranational, long-range causes is deliberate. The reason is that the arguments and counterarguments that can be made in connection with the latter too often cancel each other out. The alliance system, for instance, did contain a major danger of escalation; large nations, as has often been pointed out, were likely to be drawn into the quarrels of their lesser allies. Yet, to this one can reply that in the first place, alliances were not that binding in 1914; the Italians certainly did not think so. And one might add that if only the alliances had been firmer, if only, let us say, the Austrians had been totally certain that an attack on Serbia meant an attack on Russia, war might never have come that year.

Or there is the problem of imperialism. It is easy enough to show that it contributed to national antagonisms and to the atmosphere of violence in Europe and overseas. Yet when 1914 came, some of the fiercest colonial antagonists of former years found themselves fighting on the same side, as in the case of Britain and France, or of

* *Philip of Spain wept, when his fleet
Had sunk. Did nobody else weep?*
—Ed.

Britain and Russia. As for economic rivalries, these greatly added to the ill humor of Europe, but divergent national interests in the field of commerce did not make for armed conflict; in times of crisis, 1914 included, businessmen on all sides were among the strongest advocates of peace.

As far as the roles of the press, of the arms race, or of militarism are concerned, the arguments and counterarguments may not balance each other quite so neatly. But what is worth saying here is that problem-free ages are a myth, and that all these long-range factors were part and parcel of the mood and the realities of early twentieth-century Europe. This was the world in which the nations and their leaders had to operate, and the truly significant question is how well they did so—in the nonmythical, nonideal continent they jointly inhabited.

On the other hand, history, in Pieter Geyl's fine phrase, is an "argument without end," and another decade, or another year, may well see the rediscovery of the importance of the forces and trends so easily dismissed here.

France and Britain

The nation that, all these many decades later, can still be held least responsible for the outbreak of the war is France. This is so even if we bear in mind all the revisions of historical judgments, and all the revisions of these revisions, to which we have now been treated. And it is so even if we use Fischer's approach and ask ourselves just what the aims of France were in the years that preceded the war and after. Now it is true that some of the things that some of the French were making a bid for entailed the risk of war. More than a generation after Frankfurt, a majority of Frenchmen still had not reconciled themselves to the loss of Alsace and Lorraine. Poincaré and his friends were still pursuing what Boulanger had, except that they were doing so with greater intelligence, patience, tact, and skill, and hence with greater effectiveness. The desire to undo the decision of Frankfurt was as powerful a motive force in France's system of alliances as any. Germany, to put the matter differently, did not wish for any territorial change in Europe between 1871 and 1914; France did. It was equally true that during the July crisis, France failed to urge restraint on Saint Petersburg. One cannot very well indict the Germans for their blank check to Austria without noting that the Russians held a similar piece of paper from France.

Yet how tentative and cautious the bid to recover the lost provinces was! When we consider the restraints that the French were imposing upon themselves in the pursuit of their aims, how minor the responsibility of France must appear. The French might mourn Strasbourg, but they were plotting no war to retake it. Even the most irreconcilable groups of Frenchmen were organizing no Pan-Gallic movements; there was nothing in France to compare, for ambition and folly, with either the Pan-Slavs or the Pan-Germans. Also, all speculations about France's ultimate objectives have about them a certain irrelevancy. Perhaps France would, some day, have fought to avenge Sedan, perhaps France would not. We will never know. The fact is that the French, in August 1914, did not go to war for Alsace, but because the Germans, lacking the political imagination and the diplomatic skill to keep France neutral, first presented an unacceptable ultimatum and then began to march on Paris.

The French, in 1914, entered the war because they had no alternative. The Germans had attacked them. History can be very simple at times.

But if the French had no choice once the Schlieffen Plan had gone into effect, the British did. (The British public certainly thought so, and so did several members of the government.) What, then, was Britain bidding for in 1914? That question seems to matter more today than the point, discussed at such length in the twenties and thirties, of whether the British had given to the Germans sufficient notice of their intent to protect Belgium. That whole argument—and it includes the implication that if only the British *caveat* [had] been stronger, the Germans might have acted with greater restraint—strikes us as fairly unreal today. For no matter what Grey's precise words, or what his silences, any responsible German statesman must have known that it was a matter of vital interest to Great Britain whether France survived as a power, and who would control the channel ports of Belgium and France. The implications of the Entente Cordiale, and the very plain provisions of the Treaty of 1839, were quite sufficient warning here.

No, let us consider the British bid instead. What was involved here was no sudden, novel move, but something quite long-range. There had taken place, in the half-century or so before the war, a tremendous expansion of British power, accompanied by a pronounced lack of sympathy for any similar ambitions on the part of other nations. If any nation was compensation-conscious, it was Great Britain; if the Austrians wished to occupy Bosnia, for instance, then the British must have Cyprus. Even without this particular diplomatic gambit, the British, between the 1870s and the turn of the century, were adding, adding, adding to their empire: Burma, Egypt, Uganda, Somililand, Kenya, Zanzibar, Rhodesia, the Boer Republic, all were flying the Union Jack. If any nation had truly made a bid for world power, it was Great Britain. In fact, it had more than bid for it. It had achieved it. The Germans were merely talking about building a railway to Baghdad. The Queen of England *was* Empress of India. If any nation had upset the world's balance of power, it was Great Britain.

The usually more modest appetites of others, however, were a different matter. That the French in Morocco or the Germans in South West Africa were doing quite as well as colonizers as were the British in Uganda was something that seemed very difficult to perceive through the London fog. British territorial acquisitions were a part of the progress of mankind; those of others were a menace to world peace and civilization. Russia's desire for access to the Mediterranean was a provocation; "Britannia Rule the Waves" reflected a noble and natural sentiment.

After the turn of the century, this attitude was directed with special force at Germany, although it was seldom made clear just what the Germans were to do with all *their* excess energy. Some of the British documents of the period convey an impression of near-hysteria in the face of a rising Germany, reaching from a British admiral's simple suggestion to sink the German fleet without warning to the more erudite memoranda of some of the senior officials of the foreign office decrying the German menace. Unfortunately, if one nation imagines for long enough that another is a menace—"the natural enemy" was Sir Eyre Crowe's phrase—the likelihood is strong that the other nation will some day have to play the role it has been assigned.

Such a judgment does not exculpate the Germans, who had been willing to endorse a Balkan war that clearly contained the risk of a war in the West. As far as Great Britain's direct responsibility for the final crisis and the outbreak of hostilities is concerned, it is indisputably less than Germany's. It was units of the German army, not of the British navy, who were sending shells into Belgium. Before the guns had been moved into position, however, it can scarcely be said that the British did much better in restraining the Eastern member of the Triple Entente than they would accuse the Germans of doing vis-à-vis Vienna. "Will to war" is too grand and at the same time elusive a term to use with any degree of comfort, but what do we do about the memory of what would happen a quarter of a century later? In 1938, when the British definitely did not wish war, their prime minister would hurry to Germany three times within the space of two weeks and negotiate peace under terms far worse than those of 1914 with a leader infinitely more dangerous than the Kaiser in his most Wagnerian moods. The lamps were not "going out" (Lord Grey's celebrated figure of speech) in 1914. Many people, the author of the phrase included, were helping to put them out.

Russia and Germany

What, though, of Russia's will to war, or rather of the willingness to accept war as a possible means of policy? Here, too, our emphasis today may profitably be shifted away from some earlier assumptions. The Russian response to the Austrian threat against Serbia, as we know, consisted not only of mobilization against Austria, but against Germany as well. Here, the argument went, was Russia's major responsibility for the war. She was the first great power to mobilize. Not only that, but the manner of her mobilization frustrated all hopes for localizing the conflict; what could the Germans do but react with military means. And above all, the Russian decision came at a time when mobilization was understood to equal war.

Today, the argument seems only partly valid. For mobilization did not automatically have to mean war—except to the Germans, that is, for whom each minute counted lest the Schlieffen Plan was to fail. For every other nation, peaceful alternatives existed even after the men had been called to arms.

Not that the old argument was wholly irrelevant. For the Czar and his advisers, by their behavior at the end of July, indicated very plainly that they were perfectly well aware that mobilization, while not war, was more than a symbolic show of strength and was bound to be interpreted as an act of war by Germany. Then why did they go ahead with it? Because, and here again we owe much to Fischer and his approach of looking at a nation's boldest dreams, it was a question of the whole thrust of Russia's foreign policy over the decades that preceded Sarajevo. The year 1914 was not the first time that Russia refused to rule out the possibility of war in the pursuit of certain long-range aims. Since the middle of the nineteenth century Russia had been involved directly in two wars—the Crimean War and the War of 1877–1878—indirectly in two more—the Balkan Wars of 1912 and 1913—and, directly or indirectly, in crises too numerous to list, all with the intent of weakening the empire of the Sultan to the benefit of that of the Czar. It was a policy that acted as an irritant to Austro-Russian relations; threats to one's survival tend to annoy. Yet the Russians persisted. It was Russia rather than Austria who was the expansionist power in southeastern Europe. The Annexation Crisis was the exception, not the rule. Under ordinary circumstances, Austria had considerably more to fear from Russia's Balkan ambitions than Russia had from Austria's, even if we add the reservation that, customarily, Russian official policy was more restrained and rational than some of the truly extravagant Pan-Slav spokesmen would have liked. Customarily, for in July 1914, as it had on some previous occasions, the borderline between Pan-Slavism and government policy once more became blurred. If Serbia chose to resist Austria's demands, then Russia would support its Slavic brethren. The story of Germany's "blank check" to Austria is well known, but the Russians were doing no better at counseling caution on Belgrade. On the contrary, Saint Petersburg was giving Serbia as much reason to rely on Russian support as Berlin was giving Austria to rely on that of Germany.

Perhaps the Russians had no real choice. Caution would have equaled surrender, and 1908 was too recent a memory. This time, the alternative to active military aid might indeed have been a grave diminution of Russian influence, not only in Serbia but throughout the Balkans. Certainly the Austrians had had no reason to assume that Russia would merely look on, let alone look the other way, while they were shooting their way into Belgrade. Though if we say that, must we not in fairness add that the Russians had no more right to expect the Germans to acquiesce in a Habsburg fiasco?

Here it is, the question of German guilt. How do we deal with it, after Fischer? We deal with it in large part as nonrevisionist historians have before—by simply saying that German responsibility for

1914 goes back at least to the 1890s, to the whole conduct of German diplomacy after Bismarck. The master's touch was shown by moderation, the touch of his successors by what Bismarck had accused post-Cavour Italy of: a large appetite and poor teeth. And to what did Germany's appetite really run after 1890? To "world power," to rivalry with Britain, to a German Central Africa, to security against France? None of these policies had been thought through. Activity there was aplenty; what was lacking was a sense of purpose.

By 1914, as a result of all this ill-directed energy, a new specter had come to haunt Europe, the specter of *furor teutonicus*. German behavior in the final crisis certainly did little to banish it. The list of German blunders is an all too familiar one: the blank check to Austria; the failure, once it had become plain that an Austro-Serbian war was likely to become European in scope, to search for a compromise with every last ounce of energy; the final triumph of the military over the political rationale with the invasion of Belgium and France. "During the whole crisis prior to August 4, 1914," writes a historian [Hajo Holborn] whose sympathies are anything but anti-German, "not a single constructive move was made by Germany to stave off the impending disaster."

The list is familiar, so familiar that we need to pause and see if there is not another side to it. Just what were Germany's motives in 1914? Was it really a bid for world power that impelled the Germans to court catastrophe?

Actually, Germany's motives were far less sinister than this, though that makes them no more wise. Motives, of course, are seldom unambiguous or simple, but two great desires seem to dominate Germany's actions. One was to maintain the Austrian alliance. The other was to use the Sarajevo crisis to register a spectacular diplomatic victory, to break what Berlin considered the noose of Allied encirclement. As for the defense of Austria, it was not only that the Germans were afraid, as has been said often enough, of losing their last ally. It was also that they feared that if Austria failed to cope with the crisis posed by Franz Ferdinand's assassination, the country would be finished as a great power. "We must maintain Austria proper," was the way Bethmann Hollweg put it in the summer of 1914. "Were Russia to unleash the South Slavs, we would be lost." As for the concurrent diplomatic coup, the Germans felt, and rightly so, that their luck was running out, that their prestige had seldom been lower, and that they faced an overwhelmingly hostile Europe. A show of strength—and on an issue where moral right appeared to be on their side, as it did after Sarajevo—might radically alter the situation. Bethmann's response to Sarajevo "was determined by what he had long thought was Germany's precarious position, not by the immediate effects of the assassination itself. Sarajevo unrequited would worsen Germany's situation; Sarajevo properly exploited might lead to a dramatic escape from that situation." Or, to quote the German chancellor himself: if the gamble should succeed, "if war does not break out, if the Tsar is unwilling or France, alarmed, counsels peace, we have the prospect of splitting the Entente."

Too many ifs, we know. And besides, the German gamble was based on two major miscalculations. One was that Austria would act quickly, would "move immediately in the wake of the murder." There would thus be "a rapid *fait accompli,* and afterwards friendship toward the Entente." The other was that the worst risk the Germans were able to imagine was that of a limited, local war.

It was these two miscalculations that account for Germany's fearful part of the responsibility. These and the Schlieffen Plan, of course, which inevitably spread the war once the Austrians had made their leisurely move against Serbia, and the Russians would not be deterred from coming to that country's aid. And as the gamble started to go wrong, the diplomats found that there was no way to withdraw their stakes. What had begun as a diplomatic move (admittedly a risky one) had passed, in the nature of things, into the hands of the generals. "We have lost control and the landslide has begun" [Bethmann, July 30].

It is here that Germany's guilt lies, not in dreams of world domination. It lies, to repeat, in risks taken that were immeasurably too high; in allowing military planners to dictate policy; and beyond that, in the general amateurishness that marked the nation's diplomatic behavior in the quarter-century before Sarajevo. These things were quite bad enough. There is no need to add imaginary sins to real ones.

Austria, Some Bosnians, and Serbia

But how had the Germans become involved in the first place? Through a minor and obscure Balkan quarrel? Yes, if by obscure we mean that it was insufficiently understood by outsiders, and by minor that no vital interests of the great powers were involved. To the two nations directly affected, however, to Austria and Serbia, few crises could have mattered more, or been clearer in their implications, than Sarajevo. And both nations behaved with great recklessness in 1914.

We have stood stooped over for too long now, searching for the underlying causes of the war. We have become so involved in subtleties that the obvious has sometimes escaped us; we have not seen the forest for the roots. The obvious fact is that the issue that led to Verdun and Versailles not only was Austro-Serb in origin, but that in the immediate crisis that followed, some of the most basic decisions affecting peace or war were made by Berchtold rather than Bethmann, and by Pašić rather than Sazonov.

It is a moot question which nation practiced the worse sort of brinkmanship. Let us evade it by dealing with them in alphabetical order. As for Austria, then, it was the whole general direction of the Ballplatz's policy after Sarajevo, and the ultimatum of July 23 in particular, that invited war with Serbia, and the wider war as well. What an appalling document it was—tardy, incompetent, deceptive, designed to be rejected. Austria was setting the course, and neither friend nor foe had been allowed an honest look at its direction.

It is entirely possible, of course, to present a case for the defense. Sarajevo was no pretense; the Habsburg monarchy had some perfectly legitimate interests to defend—Serbia was a good deal closer to Austria than southeast Asia is to the United States. Surely, self-preservation is as sensible and honorable a motive as any, and the state one wished to maintain had a great deal to be said in its favor. "All my libido is given to Austria-Hungary," wrote Dr. Freud the day after Serbia's reply had been received. Austria's decision meant "liberation through a bold deed."

What alternative did the Habsburg monarchy have? Its vital interests were involved, in a way those of no other European state were in 1914; not Russia's and not Germany's, not those of France nor of Great Britain. Of all of Europe's crises and conflicts, the Austro-Serbian issue was unique in that it seemed to allow no leeway between either surrender or war. None of the others had "led to actions that produced war. They were either negotiable or repressible. The one problem that was neither negotiable nor repressible was that raised by threats to the integrity of Austria-Hungary."

Still, to understand all is *not* to forgive all. It is true enough that, as a committee of distinguished French and German historians put it in 1952, "the documents do not permit attributing, to any government or nation, a premeditated desire for European war in 1914." But Berchtold and Conrad had very much of a premeditated desire for a simple Balkan war to recover some of the monarchy's lost prestige. Did they want that war to spread? No, but the truth was that the reckless and inadequate people who were deciding policy in Vienna did not really care. This was Austria's war; perhaps only the fact that the countrymen of Johann Strauss and Sigmund Freud ordinarily made such poor villains (there would be some fairly obvious exceptions such as Adolf Hitler) allowed that simple fact to be forgotten so thoroughly.

Austria's war, and Serbia's. Two Austrian victims, seven Bosnian assassins, and no one can say to this day how many Serbian helpers. Sarajevo was more than an excuse for war. It was one of its major causes.

The assassins, in a sense, were innocents. Had he known that his deed might mean war, one of them said during his trial, he would have preferred his own death to that of his victims. But he was speaking for himself, not for Colonel Dimitrijević. Apis was a man who considered the consequences of his actions.

But to what extent did the involvement of Serbia's chief of military intelligence reflect on his government? The assassination, after all, had been planned by the Black Hand during the colonel's off-duty hours, and not by Pašić or any of his ministers. In fact, was not the crime largely a local affair, and is not the question whether any of the assassins even belonged to the Black Hand still unresolved?

Yes and no. Of course the act had its local roots. It involved Young Bosnia as much as Union or Death. Social ferment played its part along with national enthusiasm. The two great trends of nineteenth-century Europe—nationalism and the desire for reforms affecting the land—had not halted at the borders of Bosnia-Herzegovina. "I am from the village," said Princip at his trial. "Nine-tenths of our people are farmers who suffer," said Ćabrinović, "who live in misery, who have no schools, who are deprived of any culture. We sympathized with them in their distress . . . we loved our people."

Yes and no. We have complicated things too much. The roots were in Sarajevo, and they were in Belgrade. Each side was using the other. Each could do so without guilt feelings, for each loved their common nation.

Of the seven assassins, two survive to this day. One is the director of a historical institute in Belgrade, the other the curator of the ethnographic department of the Sarajevo museum. In the late sixties this author talked to both, and two questions and answers above all others remain in his mind. Who, if any, were the Black Hand members in the group? Come now, was the answer. Perhaps some, perhaps none. What did it matter? "We have many Black Hands in this part of the world." And the question of motive? He had read all the theories, and they were all of them right, and all of them wrong. "Look, we were seventeen."

We have complicated things too much. Just what, scholars have asked for years now, did Pašić know about the preparations for Sarajevo; to what extent was the Serbian government involved? Can we trust a disgruntled minister's recollections; can we put any credence in some fragmentary document intercepted by an Austrian border guard? The details are complex; the experts have never been able to agree on them entirely. Yet certain basic truths really are not very complex at all. And among them is the fact that Dimitrijević's action did incriminate the Serbian government, for reasons both long-range and immediate. That government had for too many years been tolerating or even encouraging a movement for a Greater Serbia whose aims were bound to be offensive to Austria-Hungary and whose methods were bound to be offensive to anyone. Very specifically speaking, the government in 1914 had taken no effective action to prevent the assassination of Franz Ferdinand, of which it very probably had some foreknowledge, nor had it managed to end the influence of the Black Hand, of which it assuredly had knowledge.

Not that there was anything in the least ignoble about either Pašić's or Dimitrijević's aims. The concept of a Greater South Slav State was fully as defensible as was Austria-Hungary's right to survival. Tragedy, in the Hegelian definition, consists not of the conflict of right with wrong but of right with right. But the Serbians set about achieving their purposes with a truly frightening disregard of the consequences. Here, then, was Serbia's past share in the responsibility for the First World War, one that was matched only by Austria's; Belgrade surely knew that it was set on a collision course, yet

it would not alter direction. There is, in the British files, a report from
the ambassador to Vienna, Sir Fairfax Cartwright, written in January
1913 in the wake of the First Balkan War, which sums up the entire
matter better than any later historian can:

> *Servia will some day set Europe by the ears, and bring about a universal
> war on the Continent.... I cannot tell you how exasperated people are
> getting here at the continual worry which that little country causes to Aus-
> tria under encouragement from Russia. It may be compared to a certain
> extent to the trouble we had to suffer through the hostile attitude formerly
> assumed against us by the Transvaal Republic under the guiding hand of
> Germany. It will be lucky if Europe succeeds in avoiding war as a result of
> the present crisis. The next time a Servian crisis arises..., I feel sure
> that Austria-Hungary will refuse to admit of any Russian interference in
> the dispute and that she will proceed to settle her differences with her
> little neighbor by herself "coûte que coûte."*

Had Belgrade not been bidding for a Greater Serbia, there could
have been a way out even after the Austrian ultimatum. Pašić, in that
case, could have upset all of Austria's plans by accepting the ultimatum in toto. "Such an acceptance would have made it impossible for
the Austrians, in the eyes of world opinion, to start a war, and the
few Austrian officials dispatched to Serbia to investigate the assassination would have provided a perfect spectacle of helplessness.
The claim that such a mission could not be reconciled with the
Serbian constitution cannot be taken very seriously. Worse things
had happened in Serbia that were not in accord with the constitution."

No, the reason some Serbians were willing to play the game the
way the Austrians wished them to was that they thought the prize
justified the stakes, and that with Russia's aid chances were good
that the prize might be won. Nor did they play the game at all badly.
Their reply to the ultimatum was a triumph—but it was a triumph in
public relations rather than in settling the crisis. Which was what
Belgrade had in mind. The pursuit of Serbia's aims was worth a war
with Austria. And if that war should activate Europe's alliances and
bring about an Austro-German-Serbian-Russian-French war, so be it.
No fear of international complications, after all, had been capable
of forestalling two earlier Balkan wars. Turkey was dying and now

Austria was; 1914–1918 was the longest but by no means the only war of the Turkish succession. It was the Third Balkan War.

Overlooking Belgrade stands the great Yugoslav World War I memorial, the tomb of the unknown soldier. A vast flight of steps leads up to a sort of temple where eight female figures in black marble represent the nations of Yugoslavia: Serbia, Croatia, Dalmatia, Bosnia, and the rest. On the floor, there is a single inscription, which reads:

1912–1918

Seen that way, Serbia was wholly right in the decision of July 25, and the question of "war guilt" becomes unreal and irrelevant. Of course, so was everybody right, and one wishes that Versailles had never introduced the concept of guilt. Serbia was right in wanting to expand, Austria in wanting to survive. Germany was right in fearing isolation, Great Britain in fearing German power. Everyone was right. And everyone was wrong, for no one foresaw what war would mean, either in terms of costs or of consequences. All were sinners, all were sinned against.

But then, discussions of causes, like so many other things in history, are constructions after the event. How many people, in 1914, were really that aware of all the origins of the conflict, immediate and long-range, that we abstract in leisure from the documents later? How many had thought through every move of the diplomatic game, from Princip's opening to checkmate? Not even Berchtold or Pašić. What most of them did feel—and act on—was that here was another crisis, one that contained great risks, obviously, but that might reasonably be expected to end as noncataclysmically as the diplomatic crises of the past decades had. That it did not, that this time the rhetoric of war would be followed by the reality, none of them foresaw, let alone planned. Only prophets after the event would be able to see the inevitability of arriving, step by step, stage by stage, by a series of moves and countermoves that all seemed logical, reasonable, and containable at the time, at a road which had no turns left. And perhaps, all one can truly say in the end is that World War I was a modern diplomatic crisis gone wrong, the one gamble, or rather series of gambles, that did not work out, the one deterrent that did not deter. It happens.

Paul W. Schroeder
WORLD WAR I AS GALLOPING GERTIE

Paul W. Schroeder's special field is the history of Austria, on which he has published several books and articles. Now professor of history at the University of Illinois, he pursued his doctoral studies as a Fulbright Scholar to Austria in 1956. In the article reprinted here he takes a different view of the origins of World War I from that of Remak, Fischer, and Mayer. In so doing he breaks new ground in a way that must be taken into account by any student of the subject. It is not too much to say that he has initiated a new phase in the search for the explanation of why the war was not avoided.

In a recent article, Joachim Remak argues that modern research on the origins of the First World War, led by Fritz Fischer and his students, has distorted our view while expanding our knowledge. The search for more profound causes of the war has tended, in Remak's phrase, to make us miss the forest for the roots. World War I was really the Third Balkan War. It arose from the last of a long series of local Austro-Serbian quarrels, none of which had led to war before; it involved a series of political maneuvers and gambles typical of the great power politics of that time, maneuvers which previously had not issued in general conflict. Only the particular events of 1914 caused this particular quarrel and this diplomatic gamble to end in world war.

There is much truth in this familiar view, and considerable point to Remak's criticism of an overly determinist interpretation of 1914. Yet his version appears to me as unsatisfactory as those he criticizes. This essay, without claiming to exhaust the literature or to say anything brand new, will suggest another way to look at the origins of the war, and propose a view different from Remak's, Fischer's, Arno Mayer's, and others now current.

To start with Fischer: most of what he says about Germany and her bid for world power is true. Many of his formulations and emphases are open to challenge. He is too hard on Bethmann-Hollweg and misinterprets the motives of his crucial decision in 1914. He often

From Paul W. Schroeder, "World War I as Galloping Gertie: A Reply to Joachim Remak," *Journal of Modern History* 44 (1972): 319–345. Reprinted with the omission of all footnotes except one, by permission of *The Journal of Modern History* and the author.

148

underestimates the importance and persistence of concerns other than *Weltpolitik* in German policy, and he tends to blur the difference between Germany's prewar and wartime goals in emphasizing their continuity. But these points do not destroy his main argument. From 1890 on, Germany did pursue world power. This bid arose from deep roots within Germany's economic, political, and social structures. Once the war broke out, world power became Germany's essential goal. Fischer and his students have made the old apologias for German policy impossible.

The difficulty arises in accepting the notion, implicit in all of Fischer's work and explicitly drawn by many historians as the chief lesson of it, that Germany's bid for world power was the *causa causans,* the central driving force behind the war. Fischer never demonstrates this convincingly. His case is far more informative, compelling, and reliable on Germany's policy and national character than on the origins of the war. He may be able to tell us what Germany was like without worrying much about the policies of other powers (although even here the comparative dimension is lacking). But he cannot assume, as he constantly does, that German policy was decisive for other powers without a great deal more investigation than he has done. Moreover, Fischer's own principle of *der Primat der Innenpolitik* [the primacy of internal policy] should have led him to assume that other powers would, like Germany, act mainly from their own indigenous drives, rather than mainly react to what Germany did, as he depicts them doing.

More important, the whole attempt to find a *causa causans* behind the multiplicity of contributing factors is misconceived. It is like looking for *the* driving force behind the French or Russian Revolutions, or the Reformation, or the American Civil War. Immediately, one encounters a plethora of "causes" far more than sufficient to account for the phenomenon one wishes to explain, clearly connected with it, and yet not "sufficient" in the sense that any set of them logically implies what occurred. The fact that so many plausible explanations for the outbreak of the war have been advanced over the years indicates on the one hand that it was massively overdetermined, and on the other that no effort to analyze the causal factors involved can ever fully succeed. When on top of earlier valid arguments Fischer and his disciples insist that Germany's bid for world power was really behind it all, when Marxist historians insist that the war was the inevitable outcome of monopolistic capitalist imperialism, when Arno Mayer proposes domestic political and social unrest and the dynamics of counterrevolution as decisive, and when Peter Loewenberg argues in reply that this role belongs to the fundamental drives revealed by psychodynamic theory, one begins to suspect that all these approaches, however much valuable information and insight they may provide, cannot deliver what they promise. Not only is an attempt to reduce or subordinate the various contributing factors to some fundamental cause methodologically very dubious, but also, even if it worked—even if one managed to fit all the contributing factors into a scheme of causal priority through factor analysis—this would still not give the *causa causans.* For in the breakdown of a system of relations such as occurred in 1914 as a result of various intertwined and interacting forces, the system itself enters into the work of destruction. In the process wittily described by Hexter as "Galloping Gertie,"[1] the very devices built into a system to keep it stable and operative under stress, subjected to intolerable pressures, generate forces of their own which cause the system to destroy itself.

World War I seems to me clearly a case of "Galloping Gertie." Witness how statesmen and military leaders everywhere in 1914, especially in the Central Powers, felt themselves to be in the grip of uncontrollable forces. They sensed that their calculations were all futile and that what their actions would finally produce lay beyond all calculation. Remak, appreciating this fact and rejecting the search for a *causa causans,* rightly insists that the answer must lie in the narrative and in analysis within it. But his particular answer to the question, Why World War I? is similarly misleading. True, it required certain contingent events to start a war in 1914; but this does not mean the whole development was purely contingent, with nothing inevitable about it. Europe's frequent escapes from crises before 1914 do not indicate the possibility that she could have continued to avoid war indefinitely; they rather indicate a general systemic crisis, an approaching breakdown. Remak's view of July 1914 as the one gamble that did not succeed overlooks the fact that those who gam-

---

[1] J. H. Hexter, *The History Primer* (New York, 1970), pp. 118–135. "Galloping Gertie" was the popular name for the Tacoma Narrows Bridge in Washington, which collapsed in 1940 when winds induced pressures on supporting members sufficient in turn to cause the supports to generate destructive forces within the bridge.

bled in Germany and Austria did not expect to succeed in avoiding general war.

Thus the search for the fundamental cause of World War I is futile, while the argument that the war simply happened is unhelpful. Is there no exit from the cul-de-sac? A different question may help: not Why World War I? but Why not? War was still the *ultima ratio regum.* World War I was a normal development in international relations; events had been building toward it for a long time. There is no need to explain it as a deviation from the norm. In this sense, the question Why not? answers the question Why?

More important, it points to what is unexpected about the war and needs explanation: its long postponement. Why not until 1914? This question clearly needs answering in regard to Austria. Historians continue to exercise themselves over why the Austrian Monarchy risked its own destruction by insisting on punishing Serbia. The favorite (and very unsatisfactory) answer is that this was the kind of futile, absurd action to be expected from so decrepit an empire with so inept a ruling class. In fact, the problem is nonexistent. Preventive wars, even risky preventive wars, are not extreme anomalies in politics, the sign of the bankruptcy of policy. They are a normal, even common, tool of statecraft, right down to our own day. British history, for example, is full of them; the British Empire was founded and sustained in great part by a series of preventive and preemptive wars and conquests. As for the particular decision of June 1914, the evidence is plain that Berchtold, although often wavering, resisted the idea of a punitive war on Serbia until the assassination. With the death of Francis Ferdinand, leader of the peace party, Berchtold simultaneously ran out of alternatives, arguments, and support for any other policy, and gave in. The real problem is to explain why Austria waited so long and tried so many other futile devices to stop the steady deterioration of her Balkan and great-power position before resorting to force. The idea of eliminating Serbia as a political factor by conquest, occupation, or preventive war was at least sixty years old, and constantly advanced. For over two centuries Austria had lived under the brooding threat of Russian encirclement in the south. Why did she act only in the desperate situation of 1914, with all alternatives exhausted?

A similar question arises with Germany. Why, with her powerful impulse toward *Weltpolitik,* did she fail to resort to war under favorable circumstances in 1905, or 1908–9, or even 1911, and try it only in 1914, when military and political leaders alike recognized the gambling nature of the enterprise? The same question, What held her back? applies to Europe in general. Fischer, Mayer, and the Marxists insist that the war did not just happen, but was caused. This is true, but so is the converse. Until 1914 peace did not just happen, but was caused. The wars that did not occur seem to me harder to explain than the one that did. Arno Mayer contends that we know all we need to about the European system; we lack an adequate analysis of the domestic sources of the violence that destroyed it. I disagree. We know more than we need to (although more knowledge of course is always possible and valuable) to understand in general what was impelling Europe to destruction. We neither fully understand nor appreciate the restraints holding her back, and why these gave way only in 1914.

This essay therefore deals with the question, Why not until 1914? It proposes to account for the critical difference between the system's surviving the challenges facing it and its failing to do so, by pointing to a vital element of stability within the system which in 1914 finally became destructive and generated the collapse of the system. That element, it will surprise no one to hear, was Austria-Hungary. The essay will also, briefly and sketchily, make a case for a point less trite and obvious: that a chief source of the pressures turning Austria from a stabilizing into a destructive member of the system, besides her own internal debility and Germany's policy for becoming a world power, was Britain's policy for remaining one.

The most important change in European politics after 1890, as everyone knows, was that Germany lost control of the system. Who gained the initiative she lost? For a short time, Britain seemed to; but the long-range gainers were France and Russia. Their alliance, giving them greater security in Europe, freed them to pursue world policy. Manchuria, China, Indochina and Siam, Persia, Central Asia, the Mediterranean, the Senegal, the Niger, the Congo, and the Upper Nile were the areas where Russian and French pressures were brought to bear. In every case, Britain was made to feel it.

The challenge to Britain's world leadership, coinciding with Germany's loss of control of the European system, helped conceal the latter phenomenon from the Germans themselves and contributed to their persistent belief that they could play the game of two irons in the fire and that eventually Britain would have to seek German help. Part of the challenge to Britain came from German and American industrial and commercial competition, but there was not much to be done about this. Countermeasures like imperial tariffs and economic union were likely to hurt Britain and anger the dominions rather than hamper her rivals. Besides, the main threat was to the security of the Empire, not to trade, and this danger stemmed from France and Russia. Far from threatening the British Empire in the 1890s, Germany hovered about Britain like an opportunistic moneylender, ready to offer her services at exorbitant rates and hoping for a favorable chance to buy into the firm. France and Russia competed directly with Britain and tried to drive her out of key positions. Isolated and foolish challenges like Fashoda could be faced down, but the fundamental vulnerability of Britain's position in Egypt, South Africa, the Straits, Persia, the Persian Gulf, the Far East, India, and India's Northwest Frontier oppressed the British daily. Added to this was the rise of the United States to world power and the danger of native unrest and risings in Egypt, South Africa, Ireland, and above all India. The challenges could doubtless be met, but not by the old policy, and also not by great new expenditures or tests of strength. The empire had always been acquired and maintained on the cheap, and Parliament required that it be kept so, especially now that new demands for welfare measures were being added to the old Liberal and Radical calls for cuts in military spending. As for tests of strength, the Boer War convinced most Englishmen of the dangers of isolation and the severe limits to British resources for overseas ventures.

It was therefore inevitable that Britain would meet her new problems mainly by trying to devolve some of her imperial burdens on others (the dominions or other friendly powers), and by trying to come to terms with her opponents. Bowing out gracefully in favor of the United States in the Western Hemisphere was easy and relatively painless; equally natural was the limited alliance with Japan. But the main answer to Britain's difficulties would have to be a deal with her chief opponents, France and Russia. Far from representing a great break in British tradition, such a rapprochement was the obvious step for Britain, a move for which there was ample precedent and tradition throughout the nineteenth century. What held it up was not British reluctance to break with splendid isolation—Salisbury, the great defender of this tradition, had been looking for chances to come to terms with France and Russia all through the 1890s. It was the refusal of France and Russia to make a deal on terms acceptable to Britain, counting as they did on British vulnerability to make her ultimately come to them. It took more than a year after Fashoda fully to convince Delcassé that there was no way to get Britain out of Egypt, and five years to be ready to admit it openly. Even then the British made concessions to France over Morocco which her business community there did not like at all. As for Russia, only military defeat and revolution in 1904–5, plus an expanded Anglo-Japanese alliance, finally convinced her that she must forget about putting pressure on Britain in Afghanistan. Even then, the Russians proved difficult to deal with in Persia before and after 1907.

This suggests that there is no need to bring in the German menace to explain Britain's rapprochement with France and Russia. The Triple Entente was a natural development explicable purely in terms of the needs and aims of the three powers—especially Britain. Her friendships with France and Russia were ends in themselves, vital for her imperial interests, and not means of checking Germany, and remained so. Rather than seeking friendly agreements with France and Russia because of the German threat, Britain tended to see Germany as a threat because of the agreements she sought and obtained from France and Russia. Repeatedly, before the war British spokesmen's main complaint against Germany was that she resented British agreements with other powers and tried to break them up. The great British fear was that Germany might lure France and Russia into her camp, leaving Britain isolated.

"But you forget three things," one might reply. "Britain did not approach France and Russia until she had first attempted an alliance with Germany and failed. The agreements with France and Russia were strictly extra-European and colonial in nature, and not directed against Germany; only Germany's dangerous conduct made them into a coalition against Germany. Above all, it was Germany's direct, overt, and formidable naval challenge which forced Britain to draw close to France and cooperate with Russia in Europe."

The first point errs on the facts. The story of a missed opportunity for an Anglo-German alliance in 1898–1901 is a myth, as Gerhard Ritter argued long ago. . . .

The second point, that Britain's colonial agreements were not directed against Germany, but only became so because of Germany's conduct, is true in the sense that Britain did not want to encircle Germany but to protect her empire; this is precisely my contention. It also touches on an important truth, that Germany was not in fact the prime target of Entente diplomacy—of which more later. But what about France's and Russia's purposes in these colonial agreements? Whether Delcassé's policy of trying to encircle and isolate Germany was mainly a reaction to German moves or the product of his own ambitions for France (undoubtedly it was both), his whole program, especially as it reached a climax in Morocco, was so overtly and rashly anti-German that most of his colleagues, including some ardent colonialists, warned him against it. The British knew quite well about this aspect of French policy. They chose to accept the agreement with France for their own reasons and to let Germany worry about the European consequences. As for the Anglo-Russian Convention of 1907, its fundamental presumption was that Britain would pay Russia for cooperation in Central Asia by helping the Russians improve their position in Europe, especially in the Balkans and the Straits—directly at Turkey's and Austria's expense, indirectly at Germany's. The British knew that Russia had been exerting pressure on India in great part in order to make Britain subservient to Russian policy in Europe, and they had long been contemplating using the Balkans and the Straits as lures for Russia.

It becomes even more disingenuous to claim that Britain's ententes were not intended to apply to Europe or to hurt Germany when one sees how they were used. From 1904 on, the British understood perfectly that the price of their friendships with France and Russia was diplomatic and moral support for these powers in their disputes with Germany and Austria. They gave that support even when, as often happened, they strongly disapproved of French or Russian policy. Germany and Austria, and France and Russia, respectively, being tied by firm alliances, could afford sometimes to restrain their partners and deny them diplomatic support. Britain, refusing all military commitments, had to give her friends moral support more unstintingly or risk seeing them go into the other camp.

Furthermore, even if Germany's encirclement was not a British aim, the "circling out" of Germany, her exclusion from world politics and empire, *was* Britain's goal in good measure. Grey and others made it clear time and again that the purpose of Britain's ententes, next to keeping France and Russia friendly, was to deter Germany from "interfering" and "bullying" in Asia or Africa, to keep her out of areas like Persia where she had no real business, to stop the Bagdad Railway, to neutralize the *baton égyptien,* and to teach Germany that she had to settle all imperial questions *à quatre,* before a united front of Entente powers. The *Auskreisung,* which Fischer portrays as the result of German aggressiveness and blunders, was precisely the outcome British diplomacy was bent on achieving.

As to Germany's naval challenge, all the facts, old and new, can be freely acknowledged. There was a great German naval program aimed directly at Britain and designed to promote *Weltpolitik.* It undoubtedly became ultimately Britain's greatest naval danger (after the Franco-Russian danger faded away) and the foremost element in Anglo-German rivalry. No improvement could come in Anglo-German relations without some naval settlement. But it is one thing to see the naval challenge as a real, serious issue, sufficient to itself to compel Britain to be on guard against Germany. It is quite another to argue that it primarily shaped British policy toward Germany, or that an end to the naval race would have significantly changed British policy. The latter assumptions remain unproved. The German naval challenge did not cause the revolution in Britain's political alignments, and an end to the naval race would not overturn them. The German Navy was not really taken seriously by either the government or the Admiralty until 1906–7, by which time the Entente Cordiale was a fixture in British policy and the search for an agreement with Russia had long been under way. Nor will the naval challenge do to explain the rise of Germanophobia in Britain. The anti-Germans were clearly gaining control of the Foreign Office by 1901; popular hatred of Germany was ripe with the Kruger Telegram and the Boer War. Anti-German spokesmen in the government and the press did not need the German Navy for their propaganda, though they exploited it fully. They centered their fire on the general danger of German power, the evil of Prussian militarism, and the German bullying and blackmail of Britain since the 1880s.

Nor should one ignore the fact that Germany's naval challenge was the only one among the many threats facing Britain which the British always knew they could beat. The realignment of British foreign policy came at a time when she enjoyed almost unprecedented naval superiority. The recognition in 1906–7 that Germany was now the only possible naval foe greatly improved, not worsened, Britain's strategic position; it facilitated the concentration of the fleet in home waters more than it forced it. Even the Tories, always alert for any sign of naval unpreparedness, agreed in 1905–6 that naval spending could be reduced. British publicists and a hysterical public might dream of a German invasion; Sir John Fischer dreamed of Copenhagening the German fleet and, like his successor, wanted to land 100,000 men on Germany's Baltic coast in case of war. Contrast the British confidence that they would be able to drive Germany from the high seas, destroy her commerce, and conquer her colonies with relative ease, with British pessimism on other scores—the knowledge that they could not hope to match American naval strength in the western Atlantic or Japanese in the Far East, and that the only long-range answers to the problems of Egypt and India were deals with France and Russia. Of course the British were angered by Germany's naval challenge; it was expensive, gratuitous, and worrisome. But they never doubted they could meet it; it had its domestic and foreign policy uses; it was much easier to get money voted for ships than for men and supplies to defend the Northwest Frontier. All in all, it was a price Britain was willing to pay for the friendship of Russia and France, although she would have preferred not to pay at all.

Above all, no naval agreement would have ended Anglo-German rivalry or caused Britain to abandon the anti-German coalition. To be sure, Germany demanded an unacceptable price for a naval agreement, Britain's promise of neutrality in continental war. But then Britain was never willing to pay for a naval agreement, except possibly with the poisoned fruit of a colonial agreement at Portugal's or Belgium's expense. If a naval agreement were concluded, the British would say, the improved atmosphere and friendly feelings it would produce would facilitate future amicable agreements on subjects of mutual interest—which is diplomatic language for "No concessions." In fact, Nicolson, Hardinge, Crowe, and other influential foreign-policy leaders were deathly afraid of a naval agreement. As Hardinge argued, the Russians "must not think for a moment that we want to improve our relations with Germany at their expense. We have no pending questions with Germany, except that of naval construction, while our whole future in Asia is bound up with the necessity of maintaining the best and most friendly relations with Russia. We cannot afford to sacrifice in any way our entente with Russia—even for the sake of a reduced naval program." Grey constantly reassured

France and Russia that no agreement with Germany, naval or other, would disturb Britain's existing friendships, and he meant it.

If one needs further evidence that an end to the naval threat would not change Britain's basic policy toward Germany, the secret Anglo-Russian naval talks of June 1914 over cooperation in the Baltic and the Mediterranean supply it. . . . At a moment when better relations with Germany seemed uniquely possible, and when Grey believed such relations would be vital to prevent war over the Balkans, Britain was willing to destroy this hope (for these talks, like the similar ones with France, had little chance to remain secret and did not), to risk creating a grave new strain with Germany, to promote Russo-French hopes and German fears of a full Anglo-French-Russian alliance, and to deliver the best possible propaganda to navalists in Germany for resuming the naval race—all in order to avoid disappointing the Russians. This marks a high point in the British appeasement of Russia that had been going on for fifteen years, and proves further that the *raison d'être* of British policy was her ententes with France and Russia, regardless of what Germany did, just as Germany was determined to try for world power regardless of what Britain did, and that rivalry with Germany was a price Britain was willing to pay for the sake of these ententes.

"Very well," someone will say, "what of it? Britain was simply playing the game by the normal rules. Was she supposed to have appeased Germany instead? What possible concession would have done any good? In any case the anti-German coalition Britain joined was a loose, defensive one which never would have caused war unless Germany tried to break it by force, which she did. Far from refuting the Fischer thesis, you have made it more plausible. Faced with the impossibility of achieving world power and standing by peaceful means, Germany chose war. Rather than condemning British policy, you vindicate it. For whatever her motives (and what power ever acts for motives other than self-interest?), Britain was preserving the European balance of power against the unmistakable threat of German domination. That this defense was desperately needed, two world wars would seem to give adequate proof."

The argument is tenable, provided its basic premises are accepted. If Germany's main activity was her pursuit of world power; if, further, the great problem for Europe was how to cope with Germany's growing power; if the main aim of British policy, whatever its ulterior motives, was to preserve a balance of power in Europe, and the chief effect of British policy was to restrain German ambitions, then British policy was justified regardless of its motives and even of its outcome. In pursuing her own interests, Britain was also upholding the best interests of Europe as a whole, and of peace.

But in fact the premises are unsound. Of course Germany played world policy; so did every other power that could, and some that could not. The point is how Germany played it. Somehow' Fischer never quite succeeds in explaining the contrast between the remarkable growth of Germany's power and wealth and her uniform failure to translate that power into corresponding diplomatic, political, and territorial gains. Even a small power like Belgium, or a would-be great power like Italy, could emerge from the imperialist scramble with impressive gains; Portugal and Holland could consolidate their possessions while hungry great powers looked on. But Germany ended up with little more than Bismarck had already gained in 1884–1885, and this at the cost of weakened alliances and a ruined European position. It will not do to explain this failure simply by German aggressiveness and blunders. Who could be more aggressive and commit more blunders than Imperial Russia? Yet she survived a disastrous war, revolution, and bankruptcy and emerged by 1914 with her alliances stronger than ever and her expansion once again under way. Nor will it do to cite Germany's inconsistency, her repeated failure to know what she really wanted. For the point is that no matter what Germany tried, she lost. She lost ground in Morocco when she remained passive and waited for France to come to her; she lost ground when she tried standing up for the principle of the open door; and she lost further ground when she tried to pound her fist on the table and demand compensations. Whether she tried to challenge Britain or France or Russia, or (as she did repeatedly) tried to win their friendship, she always finally succeeded in tightening the Entente against her.

The main reason for Germany's failure is not ineptness and aggressiveness, or her late start in *Weltpolitik,* or even unfavorable geography, although these are involved. It is that Germany could not pursue *Weltpolitik* all out. Each of the Entente powers could carry on a world policy without directly overthrowing the European system (although their imperialism indirectly undermined it). They could even, as the British did, indulge in the flattering belief that *their* world policy sustained the European system and made it work. But an unrestrained *Weltpolitik* by Germany, as the Germans were forced to recognize, was bound to isolate her and destroy the system upon which she had to rely for security as much as upon her army. Thus the exigencies of continental policy repeatedly imposed themselves upon Germany and restrained her.

This explains what most needs explaining about prewar German policy. The problem is not, as is often imagined, one of accounting for her reckless conduct in terms of her aggressive, imperialist character and aims. It is one of accounting for the surprising moderation of German policy until 1914, in view of her aggressive character and aims. It is clear that the Entente powers were counting upon Germany's desire for peace and exploiting it; even Germanophobes like Eyre Crowe insisted that she would back down before a firm front. The restraints lay, of course, not in Germany's policy or character or the supposed peace party at Berlin, but in the position and role the system forced upon her—which made it all the more important for the Entente not to overstrain the system holding her back.

The contradiction between what Germany wanted to do and what she dared do and was obliged to do accounts in turn for the erratic, uncoordinated character of German world policy, its inability to settle on clear goals and carry them through, the constant initiatives leading nowhere, the frequent changes in mid-course. It is commonly said that after 1890 Germany played the game of international politics like a plunger on the stock market, always looking for quick short-term gains. The truth is worse than this. Germany played it like a plunger looking for quick gains without making any investments, a gambler trying to win without betting. The Germans were always hoping to be paid for doing nothing, merely for being where they were; expecting to be feared and to have their interests respected because of the power they possessed but dared not exert. They wanted Britain to pay them in Africa for the trouble Germany refrained from causing Britain with the Boers. They wanted Russia to pay for benevolent German neutrality during the Russo-Japanese war, and Britain and Japan to pay for plain German neutrality during the same war. Russia and Britain were supposed to do something for Germany on account of her not penetrating Persia, and France likewise if Germany did not cause more difficulty over Morocco. The British ought to concede Germany something if she stopped building more ships. Disappointed, the Germans wondered with querulous self-pity why everyone was against them—the same mood they had often expressed before unification, and which would become the national disease after 1918.

Of course German restraint was not worthless to other powers, often it was invaluable. Russia was extremely lucky to have Germany and Austria-Hungary covering her rear in 1904–5, and the Russians knew it. But no one pays for such services when they can be had for nothing, especially since it was not too hard to see that the real reason why Germany refrained from causing more trouble was that she dared not do so. Like it or not, she was bound to her alliances and to her central European position. Even Italy had more freedom for *Weltpolitik* than she, and used it. For the Entente powers and Italy, alliances were primarily associations for profit; for Germany and Austria, they were of necessity associations for security.

Nor can one agree without serious reservations even to the universal assumption that British policy was directed toward maintaining a European balance of power. Of course it was in one sense: Britain wanted to keep Germany from dominating the continent by either overpowering France and Russia or luring them into her camp. This was entirely legitimate and necessary, but it alone is not enough to make Britain's a real balance-of-power policy. For, quite apart from some general reservations one may have about the whole character of British equilibrist thought, the important point is that the British neither recognized nor did anything about the most critical threat to the European balance after 1900, but helped make it much worse. The immediate threat to the balance in 1914 was not German power. That danger existed, but it was under control, so far as it could be by peaceful means. The impression everywhere in Europe was that the Entente powers, especially Russia, were gaining the upper hand. The greater danger stemmed not from German or Russian power but from Austrian weakness. One of the few incontestable points in balance-of-power theory is that preserving the system means preserving all the essential actors in it. Equally obvious, nothing is more likely to occasion a major war than a threat to the existence or great-power status of an essential actor. Whatever the underlying causes of the nineteenth-century European wars may have been, they were all touched off by a violent reaction from some declining or threatened essential actor to a menace to its existence, essential interests, or prestige. This was true of Turkey in 1853, Austria in 1859 and 1866, France in 1870, and Austria in 1914. Long before 1914 it was obvious that Austria's existence was threatened. Everyone saw her as the next sick man of Europe after Turkey. The British virtually wrote off Austria as a great power by the mid-1890s. In 1899 Delcassé tried to reach agreements with Russia and Italy in the expectation of her impending demise. From 1908 on almost everyone anticipated that the long-awaited general war would probably arise over a Russo-Austrian quarrel involving Serbia. From 1912 on the Russians and Serbs repeatedly told their Western friends that Austria's collapse was imminent, and that they intended to have the lion's share of the remains.

Yet Britain's "balance-of-power" policy entirely ignored this immediate danger, and served actually to increase the threat from Germany as well. Germany ultimately might well have gone to war for world power (although she passed up chances earlier); but she was virtually bound to accept war, even provoke it, rather than let Austria go under and thus lose her last reliable ally. This was not a matter of Germany's ambitions, but of her vital interests, as the British well knew.

Once again, even if this trite contention is true, what of it? Was Britain to blame if Austria in 1914 decided to commit suicide out of fear of death, and Germany decided to join her, or rather pushed her into it? Were the Entente powers supposed to sacrifice their interests to save a rival power from succumbing to its own internal weaknesses?

As it happens, the theoretical answer to both these rhetorical questions is yes. A real balance-of-power policy would have required from the Entente precisely such a policy of restraint for themselves and controlled support for Austria, just as maintaining the Near Eastern balance had always required the powers to support Turkey, not exploiting her weaknesses or seeking individual gains. It indicates the inherent contradictions of balance-of-power politics that the actions it promotes, which its proponents consider normal and natural, actually serve to undermine the balance rather than maintain it. But there is a practical answer more important than the theoretical one. The threat to Austria's existence, which I would argue was primarily international rather than internal in character, was a product in great part of Entente policy. As a result of the preoccupation of diplomatic historians with motives and aims instead of effects, both German and Entente policies have always been discussed almost exclusively in terms of the German problem, when in fact their effects were far greater on the Austrian problem. The best answer to the German encirclement myth is not that Entente policy was really moderate and unprovocative; there has been too much whitewashing of British, French, and especially Russian policy in this whole debate. The answer is rather that the Entente really encircled Austria rather than Germany. Of course Germany was hemmed in and constrained. But she still had allies she controlled or strongly influenced, neutral states still leaned her way (Denmark, Sweden, Holland, Switzerland, Turkey), and she was still inherently so strong that no one wished to challenge her directly. If her bid for world power was frustrated, the more modest aim of eventually loosening the rival coalition and insinuating herself into Britain's favor was not foreclosed. Grey resisted all pressures from France, Russia, and the Foreign Office to turn the ententes into alliances, and may even have entertained the hope ultimately of bringing a chastened and more moderate Germany into the Triple Entente, as the Radicals urged.

Austria, in contrast, was hopelessly encircled by 1914 and knew it. Russia, supported by France, was forming a new Balkan League around Russia's protégé and Austria's worst enemy, Serbia. Rumania was defecting, Bulgaria was exhausted and wavering under strong Russo-French pressure, Turkey was leaning toward Russia, Italy was cooperating with Russia in the Balkans; even Germany was a wholly unreliable support politically, and Austria's chief competitor economically in the Balkans.

This isolation and encirclement resulted, moreover, principally from Entente moves and policies, always discussed as if they had nothing to do with Austria. Delcassé's policy, for example, was obviously aimed against Germany (and for a good while against Britain). But is there no significance to the fact that virtually his first move in strengthening and transforming the Dual Alliance was to seek an agreement with Russia over the spoils of the Austrian Empire, and that even after his fears of a German seizure of Austrian Adriatic ports proved groundless, he still hoped Austria's demise might give France the chance to recover Alsace-Lorraine? Who was menaced by French efforts to lure Italy out of the Triple Alliance and to get her to concentrate her attention on the Balkans and *Italia irredenta*? Not Germany; Austria. Whose vital interests and security were ultimately threatened by France's move to take over Morocco? Not Germany's; only the Pan-Germans and some ardent colonialists claimed Morocco as a question of vital interest. The Kaiser, the Foreign Office, and the bulk of Germany's military, naval, and business leaders saw it as a question primarily of prestige and honor. What the French protectorate in Morocco actually did was to pave the way for Italy to attack Turkey over Tripoli and to spread the war into the eastern Mediterranean, to encourage Russia to advance her plans for the Straits, and to promote the assault of the Balkan states upon Turkey, thus raising life-and-death questions for Austria. This was not merely what happened in the event; it was what sensible leaders foresaw and planned for, what was in good part provided for in written agreements.

It is true that Austria did not oppose either France's move on Morocco or Italy's ambitions for Tripoli. This was because, knowing that she could not stop them, she pursued the forlorn hope that, distracted by these gains, they might lessen the pressure on her, or that by supporting them she might persuade France and Italy to keep these Mediterranean moves from having dangerous repercussions for Austria in the Balkans, and to recognize her vital interests there. This policy, which had never worked for Austria throughout the nineteenth century, suffered absolute shipwreck in 1912–1914, when it became apparent that all the powers, grateful though they were for Austria's restraint, intended to make her pay for everyone else's gains, and pay precisely in the only area where she had vital interests, the Balkans.

Whom (besides Persia) did the Anglo-Russian Convention of 1907 endanger? Not Germany, whose role and interests in Persia were secondary. The agreement, as intended and promoted by Britain, served to turn Russia's attention toward the Straits, the Macedonian question, and her Balkan rivalry with Austria. France's and Britain's loans to Russia, French economic penetration of the Balkans, France's arms deliveries to Serbia and Greece, and her closing her money markets to Vienna while opening them to Austria's enemies were all intended to hit Germany, insofar as they had a political purpose; but Austria was much more directly hurt. The same is true of Russia's policy, fully backed by France, of uniting the Balkan states into a league under her direction, pulling Rumania and Turkey also into her camp. Intended supposedly to protect the Straits and Turkey from German influence, it served above all to destroy Austria's position. Even the Anglo-French and Anglo-Russian naval talks were directed as much against Austria in the Mediterranean as against Germany in the North and Baltic Seas. From 1912 on France was determined not to allow an Austro-Serb or Austro-Russian rapprochement, so as not to lose a valuable third front in the Balkans against the Central Powers in case of war.

Austria was therefore the actual target of Entente diplomacy. Results count more than motives. To a surprising degree, moreover, Entente statesmen knew what the effects of their policies would be and accepted them. But how was Britain responsible for this? It is easy to see why Russia, France, and Italy might want Austria weakened, but why should Britain, her old friend and natural ally, help undermine her position?

In fact, one can argue that Britain's policy (like Russia's and even, in certain respects, France's) was more anti-Austrian than anti-German. Although opposing German ambitions, the British took Germany seriously and were careful not to push her too far or trample her interests underfoot. They never took Austria seriously and were regularly ready to let her pay, or make her pay. Britain never encouraged France or Russia to provoke Germany; firmness and moderation were the watchwords. But from the mid-1890s on, she urged Russia to concentrate her power and attention on Europe, telling her that with time and patience she could become the arbiter of Europe—the worst possible threat to Austria. The British never liked Delcassé's anti-German stance over Morocco. But they worked to break up the long-standing Austro-Russian cooperation in Macedonia, valuable though they knew it to be for European peace, exploiting the Austro-Russian rift to promote a separate Anglo-Russian program for the Balkans and Turkey. Macedonia became the birthplace of the Triple Entente; it was supposed to cement the Anglo-Russian entente at Austria's expense as the first Moroccan crisis had consolidated the Anglo-French accord at Germany's.

The British did not encourage France to try to recover Alsace-Lorraine; they did drop repeated hints to Russia about how cooperation in Asia would eventually help her in Turkey and the Straits. Britain welcomed the Franco-German agreement over Morocco in 1909 and showed little concern as the French first strained and then broke the Act of Algeciras so recently concluded. When Austria annexed Bosnia, legalizing a situation long existing de facto and giving up her hold on the Sanjak of Novi-Pazar in the process, Britain helped promote an international crisis over the violation of a treaty thirty years old, whose relevant provision had never been intended by Britain herself to remain long in force. The British sometimes tried to calm French suspicions of Germany. During the Bosnian Crisis and after, they impressed upon Russia that she had suffered a humiliating defeat at the hands of Austria backed by Germany, this regardless of the consequences for the balance of power and future Austro-Russian relations, and despite the fact that the British knew of the prior Austro-Russian bargain over Bosnia and considered Isvolski himself largely to blame for Russia's discomfiture.

While Britain in 1911 urged France to compensate Germany generously for her protectorate in Morocco, she simultaneously encouraged Russia to form a Balkan League, including Turkey, to stop Austria in southeastern Europe. Grey rejected the idea of pulling Italy entirely out of the Triple Alliance, for fear of provoking Germany; but he welcomed Italy's cooperation with Russia and her concentration on the Adriatic, and he tried to quell anti-Italian press sentiment in Britain over Italy's aggression in the Tripolitan War. While Grey cooperated with Germany during the Balkan Wars, it was often at Austria's expense, and always with great care not to offend Russia. Although the outcome of these wars fatally tipped the Balkan balance against Austria, the frantic cries from Vienna for some consideration of Austria's position went unheeded as before....

On the eve of the war, the Foreign Office was aware of the fear prevalent in both Berlin and Vienna that Austria might collapse. Far from viewing this eventuality as a danger per se, Nicolson feared only that Russia and Germany might come together over the spoils, and urged preventing this by a close Anglo-Russian alliance. Grey feared rather what actually happened: a preventive war launched by Germany out of fear of Russia's growing strength and Austria's decline. His only answer to this was to work with the supposed German peace party under Bethmann, so as to conciliate Germany and get her to put still more restraining pressure on Austria. No thought of any action to help maintain Austria's independence and integrity was entertained. If Austria and Russia actually got into war, Grey hoped to keep Germany and France out of it—thus holding the ring for

Russia, giving her the opportunity she had wanted ever since the Crimean War. . . .

Of course there was no great anti-Austrian plot. The British did not think of Austria as their enemy; they tried not to think of her at all. They did not plan to isolate and destroy her; they simply did not concern themselves (as they never had earlier in the nineteenth century) with the question of whether the concessions and defeats forced upon Austria before the war, and the territorial sacrifices to be imposed on her during and after it, would leave her viable. Britain undermined Austria's position before the war—indeed, throughout the nineteenth century—and assisted in her destruction during it, in a fit of absence of mind, a state from which many British historians on this subject have not yet emerged. . . .

What makes Britain's responsibility for Austria's plight a heavy one, although less direct than Russia's or France's, is that Britain alone was in a position to manage the European Concert so as to control the Balkan situation. . . . Right up to June 1914 all Austrian leaders, including those aggressively inclined toward Serbia and Italy, wanted an entente with Russia. Hence the situation was not inherently out of control, but only Britain could have exercised that control. France could not have checked Russia's diplomatic offensive, even had she wanted to; she was too dependent on Russian aid. Britain did not try, not so much because she feared losing Russia to Germany, or feared renewed trouble for India, as because she saw no reason to make the effort.

Instead, she expected Germany to do the whole job both of sustaining Austria and restraining her. It is strange that the Germans have not made more of this. Most German charges against England were baseless or highly exaggerated, most German expectations and demands from Britain absurd or dangerous. But the old, long-standing German and Austrian efforts to get Britain to bear her European responsibilities by upholding Austria have a good deal to be said for them. Never mind that Germany had selfish reasons for wanting to involve Britain, that Germany herself helped greatly to create the Austrian problem, and that German support for Austria was anything but loyal and disinterested. The fact remains that German support for Austria and restraint of her and Russia helped prevent several likely general wars, and that Austria by her very existence and her policy was restraining Germany, preventing her from playing world policy with a free hand. Moreover, only the presence of the Habsburg Monarchy holding down the Danube basin kept Germany or Russia from achieving mastery over Europe. With Austria there and determined to remain an independent great power, it was very difficult for either of them to fight each other, or dominate the other, or combine for aggressive purposes. Let Austria go under, and a great war for the mastery of Europe became almost mathematically predictable. The Germans, William II in particular, had many irrational beliefs, including the apocalyptic vision of an inevitable fight to the death between Teutons and Slavs. But their fear of this contest, and the belief that Austria's impending dissolution must bring it on, were entirely rational.

The main trouble with leaving the task of supporting Austria to Germany alone was not that it was unfair or exceeded Germany's resources, but that it was counterproductive for peace. The more the Germans alone supported Austria, the more she became and was considered a German satellite, against her will; the more she and Germany, instead of restraining each other, became involved in each other's largely individual quarrels, the more Austria, despairing of finding help from Britain, France, or the Concert, would be prone to seek her salvation in violence, and the more Germany, fearful of Austria's demise or defection, would be tempted to push her into it—the scenario of 1914.

Only a commitment by Britain to use her influence with France to help keep Austria in existence by maintaining a balance of power in the Balkans and restraining Austria, Russia, and the Balkan states alike could have prevented this. Such a policy had worked with Turkey for a long time, and she was far more vulnerable, weak, backward, despised, and dispensable than Austria. But the whole British tradition went against this. Despite many fine phrases, the British never understood what Austria's function really was in Europe, and how valuable she was to Britain. . . .

Yet it would be wrong to end on this note, as if Britain were especially to blame—as misleading as the current excessive concentration on Germany, and far more unfair. The basic point is that everyone saw the central threat to the European system in the decline of Austria, and no one would do anything about it. Russians, Serbs, Rumanians, Greeks, and Italians all exploited it; the French thought only of their security. Even Germany made the problem

worse, by promoting Austria's survival not as a European independent great power, but as a German state and Germany's satellite,
and by insisting against Austrian protests that war, if it came, must
be fought as a great duel to the death between Germans and Slavs.
The British, meanwhile, did not want Austria to die, but hoped that
if she must, she would at least do it quietly. In 1914 Austria decided
not to die quietly, and once this long-postponed decision to recover
her position by violence was taken, there was no stopping short of
a general holocaust.

The only reason for laying greater stress on Britain's role here is
that objectively (although not psychologically) she had greater freedom to act otherwise and greater ability to change the outcome. The
attitudes behind it all, in any case, were universal—the same short-
sighted selfishness and lack of imagination, the same exclusive concentration on one's own interests at the expense of the community.
Everyone wanted a payoff; no one wanted to pay. Everyone expected
the system to work for him; no one would work for it. All were playing
the same game—imperialism, world policy, *Realpolitik,* call it what
you will—all save Austria, and she also would have played it had
she been able. All believed, as many historians still do, that *sacro
egoismo* is the only rational rule for high politics, that it even represents a higher realism and a higher morality, when it really is only
a higher stupidity. And so the system was bent and twisted until it
broke; its burdens were distributed not according to ability to bear
them, but inability to resist. Inevitably the collapse came where all
the weight was concentrated—at the weakest point. Two titles from
Nietzsche and Nestroy sum the whole process up: "Menschlich, allzu
menschlich," and "Gegen Torheit gibt es kein Mittel." ["Human, all
too human," and "There is no remedy for stupidity."]

Suggestions for Additional Reading

The published sources and studies on the background of World War I and the crisis of July 1914 have reached vast proportions. By selecting a few of the more general works, and perhaps some of the primary sources and monographs, a student may gain a deeper insight into the international relations and the diplomacy that preceded the outbreak of the war.

One might begin with very general surveys of the backgrounds of the war. Two Berkshire Studies in European History are good treatments: Bernadotte E. Schmitt, *Triple Alliance and Triple Entente* (New York, 1934); and Joachim Remak, *The Origins of World War I, 1871–1914* (New York, 1967). A readable survey that emphasizes the disintegration of Austria-Hungary as a factor in the coming of the war is that of Laurence Lafore, *The Long Fuse* (Philadelphia and New York, 1965).

Among the older more detailed works, that of Fay, excerpted above, represents a moderate revisionist viewpoint. His first volume covers the diplomatic story from 1878 to July 1914. In contrast is the later anti-revisionist work of Luigi Albertini, *The Origins of the War of 1914* (3 vols.; New York, 1952–1957), of which the first volume deals with the period of 1878–1914. For a thorough grounding in the years from 1870 to 1902, which saw the creation of the major alliance systems and the height of imperialistic rivalry, William L. Langer's *European Alliances and Alignments, 1870–1890* (New York, 1933) and *The Diplomacy of Imperialism* (2 vols.; 2nd ed.; New York, 1951) give a detailed account and also provide excellent critical bibliographies.

After 1890 a more detailed revisionist work than Fay's is Erich Brandenburg, *From Bismarck to the World War* (tr. Anne Elizabeth Adams; London, 1927). Beginning in 1902, and more objective, is George Peabody Gooch, *Before the War* (2 vols.; London, New York and Toronto, 1936–1938), from which an excerpt is printed above. He approaches the period in a novel way by describing the policy of each foreign minister in separate but related chapters. A particularly valuable work because of its coverage of political, economic, cultural, as well as international aspects of Europe is Oron J. Hale's *The Great Illusion, 1900–1914* (The Rise of Modern Europe series; New York, Evanston and London, 1971). The latest study is by Dwight E. Lee, *Europe's Crucial Years: The Diplomatic Background of World*

War I, 1902–1914 (Hanover, N.H., 1974), a synopsis of old and recent literature on the subject. Covering the last three years before the outbreak of the war are a first-rate work by L. C. F. Turner, *Origins of the First World War* (Foundations of Modern History series; New York, 1970), emphasizing military considerations; and Fritz Fischer, *Krieg der Illusionen: die deutsche Politik von 1911 bis 1914* (2nd ed.; Düsseldorf, 1969), upholding the author's thesis of German guilt.

Pre-war crises have been dealt with in detail by Eugene N. Anderson, *The First Morocco Crisis* (Chicago, 1930); Bernadotte E. Schmitt, *The Annexation of Bosnia, 1908–1909* (New York, 1937); Ima C. Barlow, *The Agadir Crisis* (Chapel Hill, N. C., 1940); and Ernst C. Helmreich, *Diplomacy of the Balkan Wars, 1912–1913* (Cambridge, Mass., 1938). All of them need to be revised in some details in the light of later source materials. Other outstanding events are studied by P. J. V. Rollo, *Entente Cordiale: The Origins and Negotiation of the Anglo-French Agreement of 8 April 1904* (London and New York, 1969); Rogers Platt Churchill, *The Anglo-Russian Convention of 1907* (Cedar Rapids, Iowa, 1939); and William C. Askew, *Europe and Italy's Acquisition of Libya, 1911–1912* (Chapel Hill, N. C., 1942).

On the July Crisis of 1914, in addition to the works from which excerpts have been printed above, Alfred von Wegerer, *A Refutation of the Versailles War-Guilt Thesis* (New York, 1930) is an outstanding product of the German foreign office section that directed revisionist propaganda. In opposition to the revisionist view are Pierre Renouvin, *The Immediate Origins of the War* (New Haven, 1928) and the monumental work of Bernadotte E. Schmitt, *The Coming of the War* (2 vols.; New York and London, 1930), both of which, like Wegerer, are based upon incomplete primary sources. Schmitt has somewhat altered his own perspective in his later pamphlet, *The Origins of the First World War* (The Historical Association Pamphlet, General Series, No. 39; London, 1958). Reasserting vigorously the guilt of Germany, Albertini's second and third volumes of his *Origins of the War of 1914* (cited above) go further than either Renouvin or Schmitt and at the same time, by the use of direct quotations from the documents, give the reader an introduction to the primary sources.

Although the Sarajevo crime has tended to recede into the background of literature on the outbreak of the war, the tangled story of the plot has been thoroughly studied. The two "classics" with diametrically conflicting interpretations are Edith Durham, *The Sarajevo*

Crime (London, 1925), which is anti-Serbian; and R. W. Seton-Watson, *Sarajevo: A Study in the Origins of the Great War* (London, 1926), which is pro-Serbian. More recently Joachim Remak, in his *Sarajevo: The Story of a Political Murder* (London and New York, 1959) has rewritten in readable fashion the story of the plot and what has happened to the participants. The most exhaustive treatment of the plot and the question of the guilt of Serbia, Austria-Hungary, and Russia is by Vladimir Dedijer, *The Road to Sarajevo* (New York, 1966; London, 1967). He comes to a conclusion that largely confirms the position of Seton-Watson, namely that the plot is to be explained mainly in terms of Bosnian grievances and aspirations.

Since conflicting opinions often arise from differing interpretations of key documents, serious students will want to examine for themselves some of the primary sources; but even if equipped with the necessary language facility they will not find it possible to peruse the voluminous collections of diplomatic documents published by the Austrian, British, French, German, Italian, Russian, and other governments. A good selection of documents on the July crisis, although weighted on the side of the Central Powers, is that of Imanuel Geiss, *July 1914: The Outbreak of the First World War* (New York, 1967), with lengthy introductory notes and conclusions designed to support the Fischer thesis. The German original, *Julikrise und Kriegsausbruch 1914* (2 vols.; Hannover, 1963–1964) is more satisfactory, containing over three times as many documents. The original publications in the "color books" (British "Blue Book," French "Yellow Book," and so on) concerning the July crisis have been collected by the British government in *Collected Diplomatic Documents Relating to the Outbreak of the European War* (London, 1915), and by James Brown Scott for the Carnegie Endowment for International Peace in *Diplomatic Documents Relating to the Outbreak of the European War* (2 vols.; New York, 1916).

The multitudinous memoirs or biographies of statesmen, generals, and journalists offer more enjoyable reading and greater insight into personalities and attitudes. All the leading foreign ministers of the immediate pre-war years have written apologias, except Aehrenthal and Berchtold of Austria-Hungary, but a full-length study of Berchtold has helped to fill the gap: Hugo Hantsch, *Leopold Graf Berchtold, Grand Seigneur und Staatsmann* (2 vols.; Graz, Wien, Köln,

1963). The memoirs and biographies vary greatly in value and interest. Among the best are Theobold von Bethmann Hollweg, *Reflections on the World War* (London, 1920); Prince Bernhard von Bülow, *Memoirs* (4 vols.; Boston, 1931–1932); Raymond Poincaré, *Au Service de la France* (10 vols.; Paris, 1926–1933), of which the first four volumes to the outbreak of the war have been translated and adapted by Sir George Arthur, *The Memoirs of Raymond Poincaré* (2 vols.; London, 1926–1928); Sir Edward Grey, *Twenty-five Years* (2 vols.; New York, 1925); and Harold Nicolson, *Portrait of a Diplomatist, being the Life of Sir Arthur Nicolson, First Lord Carnock* (Boston, 1930).

As yet the "Fischer controversy" is largely confined to German publications, although the third edition of his *Griff nach der Weltmacht* has been translated in shortened form, as noted in the introduction to the selection printed above. A number of essays, including comments on Fischer's thesis, first issued in the *Journal of Contemporary History* 1, nos. 3 and 4 (1966), has been reissued in *1914: The Coming of the First World War,* edited by Walter Laqueur and George L. Mosse (New York, 1966). The first two years of the debate in Germany is well represented in *Deutsche Kriegsziele, 1914–1918,* edited by Ernst W. Graf Lynar (Frankfurt/M, Berlin, 1964). To this collection should be added Fritz Stern, "German Historians and the War: Fritz Fischer and His Critics," in *The Failure of Illiberalism* (New York, 1972), pp. 147–158, an address to the German Historical Association in 1964. An interesting study, written in 1923 but suppressed because of its anti-revisionist conclusions, is Herman Kantorowicz, *Gutachen zur Kriegsschuldfrage,* edited by Imanuel Geiss (Frankfurt/M, 1967). Robert A. Kann has given the character and conclusions of the book in a lengthy review, *Central European History* 1 (1968): 383–389. Other helpful articles are Konrad H. Jarausch, "World Power or Tragic Fate? The *Kriegsschuldfrage* as Historical Neurosis," *Central European History* 5 (1972): 72–92; and Fritz Stern, "Bethmann Hollweg and the War: The Bounds of Responsibility," in *The Failure of Illiberalism* (New York, 1972), pp. 77–118—largely based upon the diary of Riezler, the Chancellor's friend.

Among the available bibliographies, an unusually informative and critical guide to the memoirs and other works by actors in the drama of 1914 is George Peabody Gooch, *Recent Revelations of European Diplomacy* (4th ed.; London, New York and Toronto, 1940).

The best single handbook for further study and research is the ninth volume of the "Clio" series by Pierre Renouvin and others, *L'Epoque Contemporaine, II, La Paix Armée et la Grande Guerre, 1871–1919* (Paris, 1953), while the most complete and detailed guide to publications in all languages up to 1941 is the monthly periodical *Die Kriegsschuldfrage—Berliner Monatshefte für Internationale Aufklärung,* edited by Alfred von Wegerer (Berlin, 1923–1941). For the recent literature, see Fischer's *Germany's Aims in the First World War;* Hale's *Great Illusion;* and Lee's *Europe's Crucial Years,* all three of which provide bibliographical lists or essays.